MOUN'.
LANCASHIRE

AND THE SOUTH PENNINES

20 RIDES IN AND AROUND THE
RED ROSE COUNTY

RICHARD PEACE

**PHOTOGRAPHS AND MAPS BY
RICHARD PEACE**

EXCELLENT BOOKS

EXCELLENT BOOKS
47 MOUNT CRESCENT
WAKEFIELD
WEST YORKSHIRE WF2 8QG
TEL: 01924-384804
FAX: 01924-363970

First Published 1996

ISBN 1 901464 00 8

Whilst the author has cycled and researched all the routes for the purposes of this guide no responsibility can be accepted for any unforeseen circumstances encountered whilst following them. The publisher would, however, welcome any information regarding any material changes and any problems encountered.

The author would like to extend his thanks to Yorkshire Arts Circus Education for all the advice and facilites made available in the production of this book.

Cover photos: Top, Bradford Fell; Bottom, River Ribble
Back cover: Clockwise from top left; Rodhill Lane, Lumb
Bridge, Lune Valley

Printed in Great Britain by
Carnmoor Print and Design
95-97 London Road
Preston
Lancashire PR1 4BA

CONTENTS

Routes marked * have a shorter or easier option than stated here; please refer to relevant map. Routes marked (C) contain a significant proportion of either canal towpath or specially constructed cycle path, particularly suitable for beginners or family groups as 'linear' outings.

INTRODUCTION

WHY LANCASHIRE ? THE COUNTY'S ATTRACTIONS.

Diversity is perhaps the most attractive aspect of the Lancashire landscape. The county border runs roughly north- south, along the edge of the southern Pennines, east of Colne and Burnley, but the routes included here make use of the whole of this natural barrier. It then swings west to include the Pennine spur containing the smooth contours of the Forest of Rossendale. Further to the north the inspiring Bowland Fells contain a large swathe of land designated as an Area of Outstanding Natural Beauty. In the west the Lancashire plain stretches across both the Blackpool and Liverpool peninsulas, providing ideal, easygoing rides for beginners and family groups. The artificial administrative border should not stop either Lancastrians or tourists to the county taking advantage of the local section of 'the backbone of England,' the Pennines. The section focused on within these pages, between the Forests of Rossendale and Trawden in the west and Hebden Bridge over the border in the east, is a comparatively low section when mentioned in the same breath as Pen-y-Ghent and Ingleborough, more northern Pennine peaks actually visible from many of the Lancastrian routes. They do however add a different, some would say more brooding, tone to the great variety of routes included.

The Lancashire hills may lack the rugged aspect of their Pennine neighbours but more than make up for this with a serene beauty, and, moreover, are generally far less congested by walkers and cyclists than their eastern counterparts. Nor is their comparative lack of altitude a problem; though Ward's Stone, at 561m(1840 ft), Lancashire's tallest summit, cannot compare to the 2,000ft plus peaks of the Dales even the most adventurous bikers will find plenty of challenging gradients. If not already familiar with it, you soon come to recognise immediately the large distinctive bulk of Pendle Hill, a familiar view from many of the routes. Pendle Hill itself cannot be separated from the flat, green valley bottom surrounding the river Ribble which it overlooks.

Nor is Lancashire without its own legacy of well-preserved villages. Downham, Slaidburn and Bolton-by-Bowland are random examples of numerous evocative rural settlements where you can while away time in idyllic country pubs after a ride.The county also has its fair share of historical interest in the form of the Pendle Witches, detailed in the Pendle Hill and

ROUTE LOCATIONS

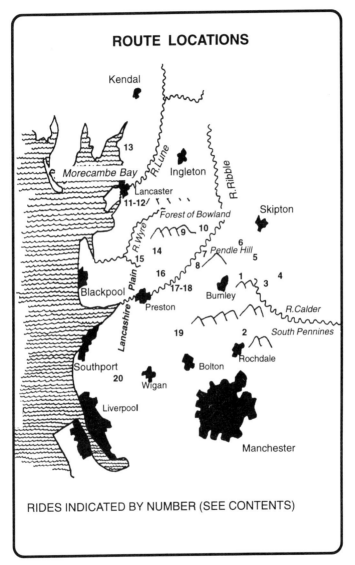

RIDES INDICATED BY NUMBER (SEE CONTENTS)

Sabden Valley routes. From the economic viewpoint, cotton earned the county a fortune during the industrial revolution and has left the many mill towns as its relics.

All this is within easy reach of the northern conurbations of Leeds, Bradford and Manchester. Road transport is no problem, the main hill areas being bounded by the M6 to the west and the A65 to the east, whilst the A59 cuts between the main Bowland hills and the smaller fells and the Pennines to the south. So why not explore this undeservedly often overlooked area ?

GRADIENT RATINGS

Gradient classifications are given in each ride:
1. Mainly flat or with gentle slopes. Ideal for beginners or children.
2. Suitable for those with some experience wishing to build up more and to increase stamina. Requires a reasonable level of fitness. There may be the occasional steep gradient or some extended moderate ones.
3. A real test. Only for more confident riders with a good level of fitness who like a challenge.
Due to the nature of the countryside, the surface of the tracks or paths may need some skill to negotiate.

Grades may be mixed to describe various sections of a route so as to give an accurate picture of what it requires from the rider.

EQUIPMENT AND TECHNIQUE

Clearly the most important piece of equipment is a bike that you can ride comfortably and safely. All the routes in this guide are really only suitable for mountain bikes, or at the very least the less common hybrid 'all terrain bikes'. You should know how to do basic maintenance and carry the following basic tools suitable for the jobs described. Because of the rougher conditions of mountain biking compared to road biking more maintenance is bound to be required:

* *Puncture repair kit ,spare inner tubes and air pump*; for burst inner tubes
* *Tyre levers;* for burst inner tubes
* *Range of spanners*; changing of wheel if not quick release. Other common adjustments e.g. if pedal becomes loose
* *Small screwdriver*; adjusting gear mechanisms.
* *Adjustable spanner*; will fit a number of bike nuts if they work loose.

* *Allen keys* ; to fit various adjustments, handlebar stem, seat post etc.
* *Chainsplitter*; this tool not only takes chains apart but you <u>may</u> be able to rejoin your chain if it breaks whilst riding.
* *Pliers*;for tightening brake and gear cables.
* *Small change and friend's phone number*; for when you are utterly stuck because of mechanical failure of bike/car !

N.B. There are special bike 'combination tools' that contain a number of the above tools and save a lot of weight e.g. Cooltool or Ritchey combination tool.

Keep moving parts, especially the chain and rear mechanism, well lubricated and free of muck. For a complete guide to maintenance see Haynes 'The Bike Book'. A helmet should always be worn (conforming to one of the usual safety standards and thrown away after an impact). I found the most other useful clothes items to be;

* Padded shorts or three quarter length bottoms depending on the weather. Special cycling shorts help to prevent saddle soreness.
* Durable footwear with a chunky sole to grip the pedal. Some pedal systems have clips or the facility to 'screw' the underneath of a sole to the pedal which can be useful to keep your feet on the pedals over rough ground. Practice disengaging your feet quickly from the system so you can use it safely.
* Good waterproof, breathable tops and bottoms.
* Waterproof cycling gloves. (Fingerless ones are very useful in warmer weather).

You heat up quickly on a bike so you should have the capability to take off and add a couple of layers of clothing and keep dry spares in panniers or a small backpack. Too much weight or too large a backpack will destabilise you.

NAVIGATION

Map and compass are vital pieces of safety equipment. If you follow the directions in the book accurately (and presuming the features used as direction finders are not altered) you shouldn't have any problems. However should you become lost these two aids are the key to finding your way back home quickly and safely. There are plenty of guides on safety in the mountains which give you accurate instructions on map reading and other important techniques. Bike computers can help in determining distances and average speed along with a wealth of other statistics of your journey. The higher up you go, the further you are from a main settlement or phonebox and the harsher the weather conditions, the more potentially vital will become your map reading technique. Its importance cannot be stressed enough.

RIDING TECHNIQUE

If you are a beginner the first thing you may notice is that riding off road up any kind of gradient is more difficult than road riding, because of the greater friction between tyres and surface. This effect varies according to the nature of the off road surface. Don't worry; take it easy and enjoy the scenery. For me the great joy of off road cycling is being able to go places and see things road cycling doesn't allow you to.

Steep downhill sections require very close control of the brakes. If you let them off for more than a second or two you can be seriously out of control. Don't try to force the bike where you think it ought to go; it will often run its own course if you concentrate on avoiding major obstacles. Relax your upper body and guide the bike; if you keep a very tight grip, hitting a small obstacle such as a stone is more likely to throw you off course. On very steep uphill sections you may be able to cut across the track or road, if it is wide enough, in a zig zag pattern. You can start to do this if you think you will have to stop pedalling heading straight up the hill. It effectively lessens your gradient and means you can take the climb in a more leisurely way. If you are on a road section watch out for traffic from behind. The key to climbing easily is selecting an easy to pedal gear **before you start the steepest part of the climb.** Also on muddy off road tracks remain seated as the weight on your back wheel will give it more grip.

The easiest way to carry the bike over obstacles such as gates and stiles is to rest the underneath of the top tube on your shoulder, but remember to stop the handlebars smashing you in the face by supporting them gently with your free hand! This is when you really notice whether you have a light bike or not.

Please keep to the tracks and ride under control and at sensible speed downhill. Mountain biking is rapidly gaining a bad name with other countryside users because of a few irresponsible riders. There have even been calls from certain quarters for legislation to ban mountain biking (also see rights of way below). Follow the code as set out below.

THE MOUNTAIN BIKE CODE OF CONDUCT.
(With the author's own additions in italics)

RIGHTS OF WAY

* Bridleways - open to cyclists but you must give way to walkers and horse riders. (*Legally they should be signposted at junctions with public roads but this isn't always the case. Also note horses, especially young nervous ones can be very scared of bikes. When they are coming in the opposite direction it's best to stop. When you approach from behind give a gentle 'excuse me' if you think the riders haven't heard you. If you scare a horse it can bolt causing injury to the rider or those nearby*)
* Byways - Usually unsurfaced tracks open to cyclists. As well as walkers and cyclists you may meet occasional vehicles which also have a right of access.
* Public footpaths - no right to cycle exists.

Look out for posts from the highway or waymarking arrows (blue for bridleways, red for byways and yellow for footpaths).

NB The above rights do not apply in Scotland.

OTHER ACCESS

* Open land - on most upland, moorland and farmland cyclists normally have no right of access without the express permission of the landowner.
* Towpaths - a British Waterways cycling permit is required for cyclists wishing to use their canal towpaths. Many sections are for walkers only.
* Pavements - cycling is not permitted on pavements
* Designated cycle paths - look out for designated cycle paths or bicycle routes which may be found in urban areas, on forestry commission land, disused railway lines or other open spaces.
* Cyclists must adhere to the Highway Code.

FOLLOW THE COUNTRY CODE.

* Enjoy the countryside and respect its life and work.
* Guard against all risk of fire.
* Fasten all gates.
* Keep dogs under close control.
* Keep to rights of way across farmland.

* Use gates and stiles to cross fences, hedges and walls.
* Leave livestock, crops and machinery alone.
* Take your litter home.
* Help to keep all water clean.
* Protect wildlife, plants and trees.
* Take special care of country roads.
* Make no unnecessary noise.

SAFETY

* Ensure that your bike is safe to ride and prepared for all emergencies.
* You are required by law to display working lights after dark (front and rear).
* Always carry some form of identification.
* Always tell someone where you are going.
* Learn to apply the basic principles of first aid.
* Reflective materials on your clothes or bike can save your life. *(Obviously this applies doubly to road sections)*.
* For safety on mountains refer to the British Mountaineering Council publication " Safety on Mountains ." *(Some of the higher Pennine and Bowland routes fall into this category)*.
* Ride under control when going downhill since this is often when serious accidents occur.
* If you intend to ride fast off road it is advisable to wear a helmet. (*I recommend it on all routes at all times*).
* Particular care should be taken on unstable or wet surfaces.

RIGHTS OF WAY

Although the legal position is set out in the code of conduct above the situation on the ground may not be that simple.

There are many minor roads shown on maps but their status is not clear from the map alone and may need further research. Bridleways may be shown on a map but may not be evident when you look for them or may be obstructed when you try to ride along them. Similarly many rights of way that exist for bikes may not be shown on the map.

These problems are solved by this guide; all routes were fully legal at the time of going to press and their legality has been researched extensively by the author. However it is still strongly recommended to take the appropriate map and a compass in case you happen to become lost. The Pathfinder maps are the most detailed showing features such as individual fields. My own directions and maps will complement these maps, although bear in mind I occasionally point out bridleways that may not be marked as such on these maps. Also in the directions reference is made to bridleway gates. For the uninitiated these are gates about a third the width of normal farm gates, designed to let the legal 'traffic' of horses and bikes through but to exclude other motor vehicles. Of course bridleways may also pass through conventional farm gates.

Please stick to the tracks indicated. In particular mountain bikers going down footpaths and private roads in some areas have caused a severe backlash against the sport and have prompted calls to parliament to have it banned !

KEY TO ROUTE MAPS

Public road	Settlement	Prominent Hills	Monument or historical feature
Road, track or path without cars	Canal	Spot Height	Rock outcrop
Line of route	River	Lake or Reservoir	Quarry

ANNOTATIONS

DIRECTION

R = Turn to the right

L = " " " left

0 = Bridleway

¶ = Signpost

MAPS AND GRAPHS

S on route maps signifies the suggested starting point

! Steep Climb (2 = very steep)

⚑ Difficult descent (2 = very difficult)

11

USEFUL ADDRESSES

Cyclists Touring Club, Cotterell House, 69 Meadrow, Godalming, Surrey GU7 3HS 01483 417217

British Cycling Federation, National Cycling Centre, Stuart Street, Manchester M11 4DQ 0161 2232244

Cycling Project for the North West, Enviromental Institute, Bolton Road, Swinton, Manchester M27 2UX 0161 7941926 A charitable group concentrating partly on facilitating cycling for the disabled but also with regional information and a topical members' newsletter.

South Pennines Packhorse Trails Trust, The Barn, Makinholes, Todmorden OL14 6HR 01706 815598 Another charitable group, this time with the aim of restoring the legal standing of ancient bridleways and making them practical for use. Members' newsletter.

British Waterways, Aldcliffe Road, Lancaster, LA1 1SU 01524 32712. Issue permits for the sections of the Leeds-Liverpool canal where cycling is allowed. It also produces useful photocopy sheets showing which sections of their various canals are open to cyclists.

Bowland Camping Barns Camping Barns Reservation Office, 16 Shawbridge St. Clitheroe BB7 1LY 01200 428366.

Cycle Hire Prices start from £12.00 per day

Dtours, Horwich	Pedal Power, Clitheroe	Cycle 2000, Lancaster
01204 699460	01200 422066	01524 381414

Tourist Information Offices

Lancaster, 29 Castle Hill. 01524 32878
Preston, Guild Centre, Lancaster Rd. 01772 253731
Beacon Fell, Fell House, Beacon Fell Country Park. 01995 640557
Clitheroe, 12-14 Market Place. 01200 425566
Burnley, Bus Station. 01282 423125
Blackburn, 15-17 Railway Road. 01254 53277

Mountain Rescue

Dial 999 and tell the operator the required service. Give the number of the phone and stay there until the emergency services ring you back. Make sure you give your location as accurately as possible.

1. WIDDOP AND GORPLE RESERVOIRS

START *Long Causeway car park ,above A646,*   **Grid ref.** *894288*
South East of Burnley

DISTANCE *26 km / 16.2 miles*   **TIME ALLOWED** *5 Hours*

GRADIENT DIFFICULTY *2/3*

TRACK SURFACE *On-road = 10 km / 6.2 miles Off-road = 16 km / 10 miles. There is a huge variety of off-road surface here, from good hard tracks to really muddy sections on parts of Duke's Cut (best avoided after rain) and everything in between.*

ORDNANCE SURVEY MAPS
1:50,000 *Landranger 103 Blackburn & Burnley*
1:25,000 *Outdoor Leisure 21 South Pennines (newer double sided edition).*

ACCESS *From the A646 out of Burnley climb onto the 'Long Causeway' after Walk Mill, through Over Town. The car park is quite obvious on the left, shortly after Causeway House. (From Hebden Bridge the car park is best accessed via Mytholm then Blackshaw Head)* **Train** *Burnley train station is about 5km from the route, accessing the route at Worsthorne. From the West Yorkshire side use Todmorden station (6km from where Duke's Cut joins the road).*

SUMMARY *This is a real tester, firstly because some of the off-road climbs are very long (the ascent to Gorple Stones) or quite muddy and steep (part of Duke's cut - see alternative longer road route on the map, avoiding this difficult section); secondly you reach a height of 420m (about 1380 feet) and even on warm summer days once at this height the wind is often strong, slowing you down considerably. It's certainly for those with some previous experience. Having said all this the scenery is quite spectacular, especially the descent towards Widdop Reservoir and the views south over the Cliviger Gorge from the Long Causeway.*

Come out of the car park and **R** onto the 'Long Causeway' road. Follow for about 3km into Mereclough and stay on the main road in Mereclough to meet a T-junction. **R** onto Red Lees Road. Shortly take the **R ¶** Rock Water

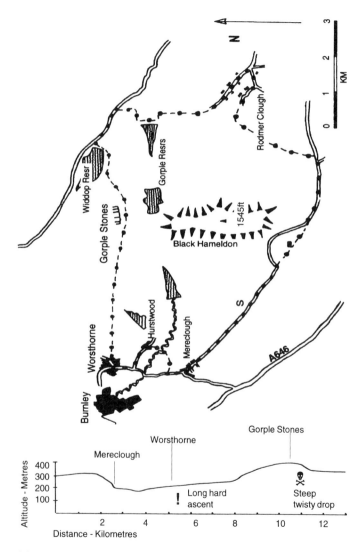

N

KM
0   1   2   3

Widdop Resr

Gorple Resrs

Rodmer Clough

Gorple Stones

1545ft

Black Hameldon

Hurstwood

Mereclough

Worsthorne

S

A646

Burnley

Gorple Stones

Worsthorne

Mereclough

Altitude - Metres
400
300
200
100

Long hard
ascent

!

Steep
twisty drop

Distance - Kilometres
2   4   6   8   10   12

14

Bird Centre and as **O**. Follow Foxstones Lane until you come to the entrance to the bird centre. Take the track down the side of the farm buildings, just before the entrance, on the **L**. Through a gate it becomes rocky and drops down over a picturesque bridge, climbing to emerge by an ancient looking building in Hurstwood. Bear **R** at this house then immediate **L** onto the main road (away from the telephone box). At the next T-junction **R** onto Ormerod Street, bringing you into Worsthorne. **R** just past the church (¶ Gorple 2 and 3/4) leads you onto the moors as the tarmac road breaks up into a stony track. Simply follow this main track for 6km until it meets the road at Widdop Reservoir. The track climbs steadily to Gorple Stones, overlooking Gorple Upper Reservoir, before leading to a steep hairpin descent towards Widdop Reservoir, following the southern side of the water and the dam wall to meet the road.

R onto this road and by the next small car park area look for **0** ¶ Lower Gorple and Colden, through the green gates. Stick to the concrete track over the eastern dam wall of Lower Gorple reservoir and follow it bending left. Just after the house on the left follow the ¶ **0 R** through green gates, climbing through another gate and straight on following further ¶**0** for Colden.

Crossing over the brow of Heptonstall Moor, Stoodley Pike monument comes into view in the distance. Descend for a couple of killometres and shortly after the track turns to tarmac road and at the first road junction take the immediate **R** at this meeting of four roads (a small sign on your right indicates you are heading for such strange sounding places as Salt Pie and Rodmer Clough amongst others). The fast undulating road leads downhill into trees. Just over the small bridge go **R** through 'hothouses' with ¶ for Rodmer Clough on the first building. At Rodmer Clough pottery bear to the left on

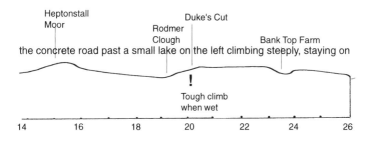

the concrete road past a small lake on the left climbing steeply, staying on the main track then hairpinning to the right. At the top of this very steep climb the track splits just after a house; take the **L ¶ 0** for Duke's Cut. The now green track levels out here before meeting a gate. Through the gate follow the fence and wall remains on the left of the field on the deeply rutted track (very difficult). At the top of this climb join a better track at a T-junction and **R**. Stay on this track (ignoring left turns) to meet the road, just past a mast.

R onto the road and continue until a left turn just after the windfarm comes into view, **¶** Shore and Todmorden. Progressing across the mouth of this road junction go onto the track **¶** as **0**. The track leads to farm buildings; bear to the right of the buildings through a gate into a field. Follow the left hand side of the field by a ditch and descend steeply in the bottom corner through a small gate to emerge by another building. Pass through the gate on your **R** just before a disused building and onto a track to the left of a house. Now simply follow this track uphill past the windfarm to rejoin the road and **L** onto it. It's now only about 1km back to the car park on the right.

ALONG THE WAY

This particular area of the southern Pennines is extremely important as a water gathering area; the Widdop, Walshaw and Gorple reservoirs were built between 1871 and 1934 to supply Halifax's water. When I did this run in the late summer of 1995 the reservoirs passed were almost empty.
*The area is also of great natural importance, forming part of **Haworth Moor Site of Special Scientific Interest,** and looks particularly beautiful in August when much of the moorland is carpeted by Bell Heather.*

Descending to Widdop Reservoir (Route 1)

2. TODMORDEN MOOR

START Bacup   **Grid ref.** 874235

DISTANCE 23km / 14.3 miles   **TIME ALLOWED** 5 hours

GRADIENT DIFFICULTY 3

TRACK SURFACE *On-road = 10km / 6.2 miles   Off-road = 13km / 8.1 miles. Flower Scar Road and the track up the side of Green's Clough are ideal mountain bike tracks; hard packed with virtually no obstacles, ideal for long scenic rides (although very probably the weather wil be colder and with stronger winds than may be apparent nearer sea level). There are one or two green lane or field sections that may be prone to muddying and may need you to push, but the majority of the ride should not present too many problems, though some gradients are very steep. Be aware the A646 is major a route across the Pennines and as such can carry heavy and fast industrial traffic.*

ORDNANCE SURVEY MAPS
1;50,000 *Landranger 103 Blackburn and Burnley*
1;25,000 *Outdoor Leisure 21 South Pennines (double-sided newer edition).*

ACCESS *Heading east out of Bacup, on the A681 towards Todmorden look for Elm Street leading to the Church on Beech Street.* **Car** *There is plenty of road parking in this area.* **Train** *On the Lancashire side the nearest station is at Rawtenstall 9km from the start of the route. If coming from the West Yorkshire side from Todmorden station take the A6033 then A681 west to join the route at the start of Flower Scar Road (6km).*

SUMMARY *Although not for the faint hearted this route gives you great views of the Cliviger Gorge. After the long straight moor ride over Todmorden Moor it's a spectacular descent to the valley floor and steep winding ascents of the nooks and crannies of the opposing valley face. There is also the opportunity to 'refuel' in the valley bottom at the Roebuck Inn.*

Go to the end of Beech Street and **R.** Just round the left hand bend take the unsigned right up a tarmac road (the turning before Windermere Road). Climb on this road staying on the tarmac ignoring rough tracks to the left and right, passing houses and climbing onto the moor as the road turns to

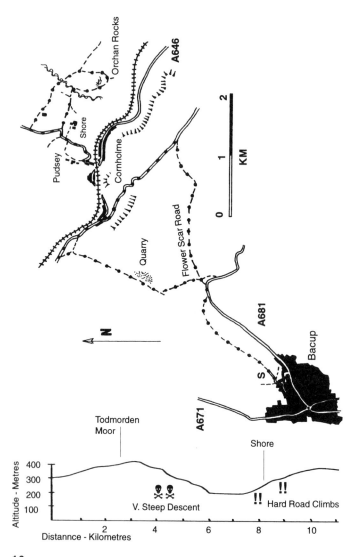

a stone track. Follow the track over the moor and descend to the main road, the A681, and **L**. Very soon, as the road bends right, go straight ahead onto an unsigned badly tarmaced track and under pylons. At the first set of track crossroads head straight on. Now on Flower Scar Road head over Todmorden Moor with great views of Stoodley Pike and the far side of the valley. Steeply descend the track to meet a minor road and **L**. This road climbs then descends steeply to the valley bottom to meet the main road by the Roebuck Inn and Tannery on the left.

R onto the main road and follow under the larger second railway bridge into Cornholme, taking an immediate **L** after the bridge, ¶ Shore 3/4 , just before the Waggon and Horses pub. At the first split by a pond on the left go **R** leading steeply uphill. At the first group of houses ignore Pudsey Road to the left and carry on climbing on Shore New Road.

Climb through Shore, past the ¶ for the Baptist church on the right and ¶s for **0**s at hairpins right and left. The climb levels out to a straighter road. 0.5 km out of Shore take the ¶ **0** to the **R**, opposite a footpath, onto a wide dirt track. Follow the track to face Lower Intake Farm and the bend left following the **0** waymark onto a narrow track, keeping the farmhouse on your right as the track then widens. Follow the track straight on through a gate, ignoring any turnings before you dip down and up to cross Redmires Water. After Redmires Water take the first track **R** ¶ Jumps Road and follow downhill as the imposing Orchan Rocks come into view. Follow the main track as it bends 90 degrees right below the Orchan Rocks to come to a gate. Immediately through the gate pick up the main track to the **R,** quite a steep uphill. Follow over the brow of the hill with the impressive Redmires Water which passes through a gorge down to the left.

At Hudson bridge bear **L** following the ¶ for Bluebell Lane. Shortly meet a T-junction of tracks and **L** to go through the gate in front of Hartley Royd building and **R** past this building. Follow this good track and in front of

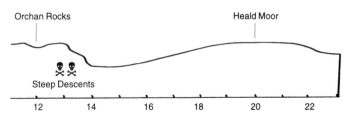

Ridgegate Farm bear **R** at the split and follow to the tarmac road and **L** to rejoin the road going downhill. Follow the road back to the main road and **R** back under the bridge on the main road.

Heading out of Portsmouth pass signs for Burnley, Cliviger and Lancashire, and on a left hand bend look for a grass track on the **L** doubling back 180 degrees uphill through trees (look for South Pennine Packhorse Trail sign on gatepost). Emerge at a stone track and **R**. Climb with superb views behind you. The track leads you into a field. Follow the rough grass track straight across and under pylons then bear left towards a disused barn. Pick up the track again through the gate behind the barn to head over the side of Heald Moor.

Approaching the colliery workings at the split take the **R** onto the higher road leading you above the workings to the left and rejoining the main track further on. There is a possible carry if the gate is locked, as you stay on the main track swinging left away from the quarry as the road becomes good quality. Follow this track down to crossroads just before the second set of pylons and **R** back to the main road. **R** onto the main road and very shortly pick up the unsigned Flower Scar Road on the **R** to follow your outwards route back to Bacup.

ALONG THE WAY

Geographical features are perhaps the most striking part of this route. *The Cliviger Gorge* stands out whilst looking across the main valley from the northern side, its pillar- like repetitive formations being formed during the last ice age by meltwater streams cutting into the carboniferous rock. Other-worldly rock formations of millstone grit such as *Orchan Rocks* are also common hereabouts. *Mount Cross* is found on turning right after your ascent through Shore. As you turn off the road onto the bridletrack the outline of this stone cross can be seen in a field to your right. Nobody is sure of its age, although it's doubtless of great antiquity. Its exact purpose is similarly obscure; one theory is that being sited at an important junction of packhorse routes it was set here by monks from Whalley Abbey to guide travellers on their way (for details of Whalley Abbey see route 18).

3. ROCHDALE CANAL

START *Todmorden town centre*   **Grid ref.** *936240*

DISTANCE *17km / 10.6 miles*   **TIME ALLOWED** *2.5-3 hours*

GRADIENT DIFFICULTY *2 with a grade 3 road climb out of Hebden Bridge. Grade 1 if you take the canal only option.*

TRACK SURFACE *On- road = 4km / 2.5 miles   Off -road = 13km / 8.1 miles. The canal side track is perfectly flat and of good surface in most places. Ideal for family outings though a little narrow. The only 'fun' obstacles are the cobbled weirs across the path where the canal overflows into the nearby Calder. See comments in introduction and summary on canal riding. The track doubling back above the canal towards Stoodley Pike is mainly good hard packed quality but becomes boggy in the later stages after rain or in winter.*

ORDNANCE SURVEY MAPS
1;50,000 *Landranger 103 Blackburn and Burnley*
1;25,000 *Outdoor Leisure 21 South Pennines (newer double sided edition).*

ACCESS *At roundabout junction of A646 and A6033 in Todmorden centre head south on the latter road. Very soon the first bridge you cross takes you over the Rochdale Canal from where you can access the towpath.* **Car** *Off-road parking on minor roads around the bridge.* **Train** *Station very near Todmorden centre.*

SUMMARY *You have two choices with this route. An easy grade 1 family run exists simply by following the canal to Hebble End (Hebden Bridge town centre is easily explored from here) then following the same route back along the canal path. Alternatively there is a much harder climb out of Hebden Bridge to follow a parallel route above the valley with lofty views over the town and valley to the west, descending beneath the local landmark of Stoodley Pike. There are pubs and cafes at the Hebden Bridge end of the canal. Be aware that at popular times there may be numerous fishermen along the canal path after carp and bream so go slowly.*

On the westerly side of the bridge over the canal, by the lock, look for the small tunnel back under the bridge keeping the canal on your right. Simply

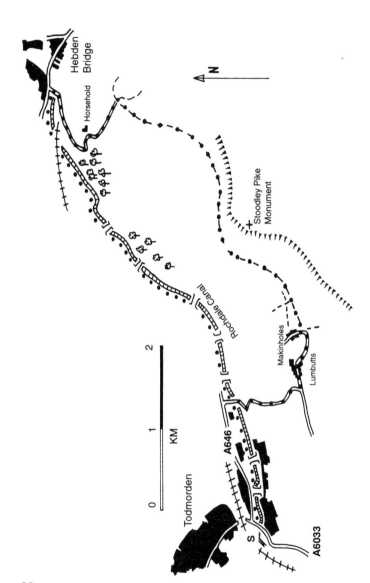

N

Hebden Bridge

Horsehold

Stoodley Pike Monument

Rochdale Canal

Makinholes

Lumbutts

A646

Todmorden

A6033

S

0   1   2

KM

stick to the canal path out of Todmorden into the countryside past various locks and under and over various bridges, for 6.5 km to arrive in Hebden Bridge.

Look out for the distinctive Hebble End bridge sloping across the canal at 45 degrees, shortly after the Stubble End pub on the left. Just under the bridge are a convenient group of cafes. Pass under the bridge and loop round 180 degrees to pick up the road over it, beginning to climb steeply. Take the first **R** ¶ Horsehold. Through woods on a very steep climb your route turns into a cobbled road. Climb through Horsehold, staying on the road as it twists left and right. At the end of a straight out of Horsehold the tarmac road stops at a gated junction with three other tracks. Follow through the gate to the **R** (unsignposted). Simply follow this main track past farms and small clusters of buildings in the general direction of the Stoodley Pike monument ahead of you. Passing beneath the steep hill up to Stoodley Pike ignore any turnings off the main track and carry on to the T-junction with a tarmac road in Makinholes.

L here and follow the road into the small village of Lumbutts. Follow the main road past the pub on the right and Lumbutts Mill (currently an activity centre for executives) on the left and over the bridge. Coming out of the village centre take the first unsignposted **R** just before speed derestriction signs, dropping steeply downhill through woods. Coming over the bridge over the canal look for a small set of steps on the **R** and carry down onto canal towpath and **R** back under the bridge, to follow the canal, keeping it on your left, back to your starting point in Todmorden.

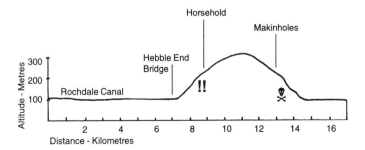

ALONG THE WAY

Stoodley Pike monument stands isolated and commanding on Higher Moor, above the Calder valley. Originally built by local subscription to celebrate victory over Napoleon in 1814, the present monument was completed in 1856 after being struck by lightening. It has a public viewing gallery 40 ft up its 120 ft height. Its purpose is radically different to traditional post world war one and two monuments which usually mourn the loss of the dead or proclaim the 'glory' of victory; an inscription on it makes clear it celebrates the outbreak of peace.

The Rochdale Canal, finished in 1804, was five years in the making and was the first canal link across the Pennines. The section covered here has been restored and is popular with all types of user, including many beautiful narrow boats which you may see passing through the numerous locks. The current programme of restoration aims to make the whole length of the canal navigable, from Sowerby Bridge to Manchester, thus linking it to the national network.

Waterfall at Lumb Bridge (Route 4)

24

4. CRIMSWORTH DEAN

START *Clough Foot car park*　　　　**Grid Ref.** *947324*

DISTANCE *14km / 8.7 miles*　　　　**TIME ALLOWED** *3 hours*

GRADIENT DIFFICULTY *Mainly an easy grade 2. A short but extremely steep drop and climb back up takes you down to the waterfall at Lumb Bridge.*

TRACK SURFACE *Off-road 14km / 8.7 miles*
Most of the track is good hard packed track on the moor tops and is well drained. There is the odd field section, but it's fairly obvious well drained green track (e.g. past Shackleton Knoll).

ORDNANCE SURVEY MAPS
1;50,000 Landranger 103 Blackburn and Burnley
1; 25,000 Outdoor Leisure 21 South Pennines (newer double sided version).

ACCESS *Heading west out of Hebden Bridge on the A646 look for the acute right turn for Heptonstall (requires you to use a turning point further down on your left). Follow the road as it climbs steeply to by-pass Heptonstall (restricted access) and comes to a split in Slack at the Zion Church going left here. Follow this road onto the moor tops, dipping in and out of the picturesque valley at the head of the Hebden Water. 5km after Slack park at the second car park, opposite the entrance gate to Gorple Lower reservoir.*
Train *From Hebden Bridge simply pick up the road through Slack as detailed above, to the starting point.*

SUMMARY *This ride gives you a chance to visit perhaps the most famous countryside spot in the district - the area around Hardcastle Crags and the waterfall at Lumb Bridge. The latter is down a steep drop but well worth the effort. There are great views above the Hebden Water valley and a nice wood section through Crimsworth Dean. Although a short run it's one you won't want to hurry. Be warned though, the area's popularity does bring hordes of visitors, especially at weekends.*

From the parking ground turn **R** back onto the road. Almost immediately note the metal gates on the Yorkshire Water road to Walshaw Dean

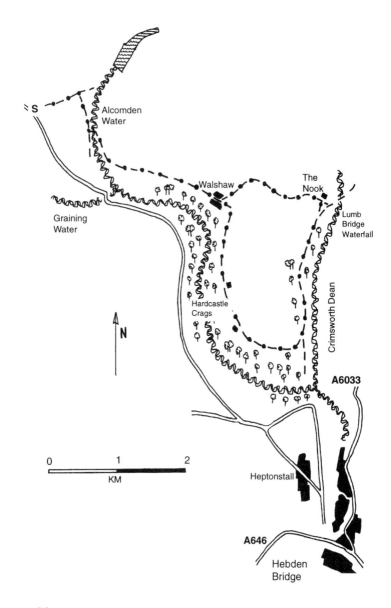

Alcomden Water

S

Walshaw

The Nook

Lumb Bridge Waterfall

Graining Water

Crimsworth Dean

Hardcastle Crags

N

A6033

0 1 2
KM

Heptonstall

A646

Hebden Bridge

26

Reservoirs, above you to your **R**. Take the ¶ **0** that runs parallel to the main lorry track (this **0** also forms part of the Pennine Way). Pass through the first gate and shortly hit a concrete road which branches to the **R** (the track ahead is ¶ footpath only and this junction marks the point where you leave the Pennine Way). Again very shortly come to a T-junction with a concrete track and **R**. At the first split **L** takes you down to a picturesque bridge. Simply follow this track across New Laithe Moor and through a gate to bring you to the small settlement of Walshaw, 2km after the bridge. From this point on the track alters haphazardly between hardpack and proper tarmac road (though with very few vehicles). Through tiny Walshaw on the main track you should spy a three-way **0** signpost. The track you have arrived on is ¶ Clough Foot. At the split ahead take the **R** track ¶ Hardcastle Crags and head towards a small group of trees. Bend right over a delightful little bridge and ignore the right split, staying straight on, ¶ Hardcastle Crags via Shackleton.

Now simply follow the obvious track as it bends through various houses and barns above Hebden Vale to your right, just being able to glimpse the top of Hardcastle Crags through the trees. Eventually enter trees at the National Trust 'Hardcastle Crags' sign.

Descend through the woods to a T-junction by a good viewpoint at a bench, overlooking the steep bank of Middle Dean. Go **L** at this junction to climb again and bear **L** at the split just before emerging out of the woods, as the climb levels out. Pass the left turn to Abel Cote farm then 'Laithe ' on the right. Pass two fields on your right after 'Laithe' then look for an unmarked and indistinct green track that drops away sharply to your **R**. Following this and bearing **R** at the first 'green lane' junction will take you to the incredibly picturesque waterfall at Lumb Bridge. **NOTE -** *It may be best to find somewhere to lock your bikes at the ruined 'Nook' building ahead*

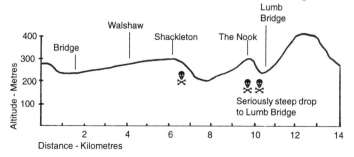

then to descend. Descent by bike is only possible for those with strong nerves and the ascent back is a very hard push. After a spot of rest and recuperation at the bridge retrace your steps back to 'Nook'.

Look for the **0 ¶ L** here, in front of the building, and take it to climb fairly steeply to a gate. Through the gate bear **L** following the **0 ¶** to follow the field wall on your left, still on good green track. Follow until a **¶** directs you through a gate and bear **R** now in a large field, following the wall on the right, keeping to the green track and gently dropping. The track eventually bends left to a gate in the far corner of the field. Follow the obvious line of the track, more or less straight through fields, to emerge through a gate into the back of Walshaw. Bear **R** through the settlement to pick up the track you arrived on, through a gate. Simply follow your outward route back to Clough Foot car park.

ALONG THE WAY

Hardcastle Crags are one of the major tourist draws of this area, indeed the whole of West Yorkshire. Although they are not accessible by bike this route passes close by and takes in some breathtakingly pretty scenery of small steep sided valleys covered with deciduous woods.

Wycoller Hall (Route 5)

5. WYCOLLER VILLAGE

START *Car Park near Wycoller village*   **Grid Ref.** *926395*

DISTANCE *15km / 9.3 miles*   **TIME ALLOWED** *3 hours*

GRADIENT DIFFICULTY *2. There may be occasional sections where an uphill push is required, especially in the winter months after rain. Reasonable fitness required but climbs are not particularly long and difficult.*

TRACK SURFACE *On-road = 6km / 3.7miles Off-road = 9km / 5.6 miles The initial climb out of Wycoller Dean is ideal hardpacked track. There is a more testing rougher surface that may become softer in winter as you approach the 'T' to turn parallel to Boulsworth Hill. Apart from sporadic soft sections the track is generally quite hard. The old 'packhorse' stone flags are still visible in places.* **Note:** *the track surface may be upgraded in the future as part of the Pennine Bridleway project. See below.*

ORDNANCE SURVEY MAPS
1;50,000 *Landranger 103 Blackburn and Burnley*
1;25,000*Outdoor Leisure 21 South Pennines (newer double-sided edition).*

ACCESS *Wycoller village lies off the B6250 on signed minor roads coming out of Colne and in Trawden town centre. There is a special visitors car park as only residents can drive into the town itself. There is a* **train** *station in Colne, about 4km away.*

SUMMARY
A picturesque village together with a moorland section that really takes you 'into the wilds' will make this a route you come back to again and again. The very long bridleway section along the base of Boulsworth Hill requires some stamina but precedes a largely genteel cruise on minor roads through Trawden village to your starting point. **Beware: gates may be locked at the Coldwell Reservoir track end** *- see legal note on pg. 32.*

Emerge from the Wycoller Country Park car park and head **R** down the road barred to road traffic and marked as a dead end. Coming into Wycoller village bend right to meet the pretty brook running past you on your right. Continue across the ford (or over the tiny double arched bridge to the left) to carry on this good road past Wycoller Hall and the visitor centre on the

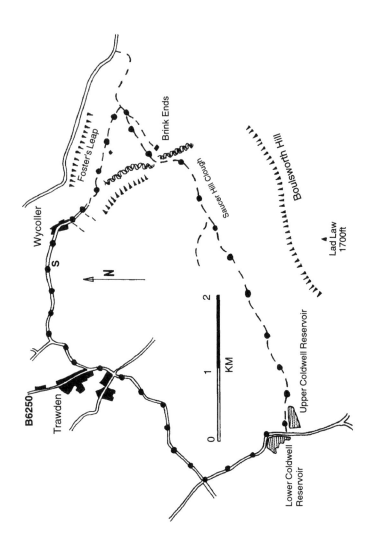

Foster's Leap

Brink Ends

Saucer Hill Clough

Boulsworth Hill

Lad Law
1700ft

Wycoller

S

N

2

1

KM

0

B6250

Trawden

Upper Coldwell Reservoir

Lower Coldwell Reservoir

30

left. Shortly after leaving the village the road turns to good quality track and passes Clam Bridge (see below) as the craggy Foster's Leap rises to your left. The track crosses the brook several times (ignore right for Dean House Farm and follow ¶s for Bronte Way and Parson Lee Farm) before coming to Parson Lee Farm itself. At the split here drop down **L** onto a green track following Bronte Way ¶. This much rougher track now climbs to reach a 'T' after passing through a gate.

Go **R** here following ¶ for Trawden (left is to Haworth Road). Very shortly your way is barred by a gate protecting the private road up to Brink Ends farm. Take the track to the right and through another gate onto a green lane running between two walls. Keep on the very wide green path and descend to the small steep sided Turnhole Clough to cross the stream in its bottom. Hairpinning steeply up the other side a ¶ guides you straight on the obvious track. Pass another sign for the Pendle Way (witch and yellow arrow).

Several small cloughs descend on your left as you climb to ride above a steep drop down to Saucer Hill Clough. Note the old packhorse cobbles revealed in places. After coming over the crown of the rise a tarmac road comes into view. Drop down onto this, heading straight on and ignoring a right turn. Simply follow this road, soon becoming track again, passing the disused buildings at Spoutly Lum and continuing on. Eventually Pendle Hill comes into view on the right and Upper Coldwell Reservoir ahead. Follow down the right side of the reservoir to meet the road at the end of this long bridleway section. (The gates at the end of this track were locked and signs here indicated you have come on a footpath but see legal note on pg. 32).

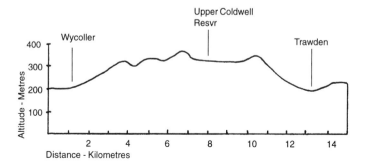

R at this T-junction to skirt Lower Coldwell Reservoir. Stay on this road ignoring first left for Nelson to climb to a crossroads and **R.** There is now a great cruise, largely downhill, to Trawden. Arriving by the church in Trawden head across at this junction ignoring immediate left and right and descend down the main street. Shortly turn off **R** ¶ Wycoller Country Park and climb to take the first **R** also ¶ Wycoller Country Park to lead you back to the car park.

ALONG THE WAY

Wycoller is centred around the ruins of Wycoller Hall, originally a sixteenth century squirearchical residence.The hall fell into disrepair in the eighteenth century as the owner died leaving numerous debts. It remained a strong and isolated handloom weaving community until the 19th century when the collapse of this industry turned Wycoller into a ghost village of crumbling buildings. Only in the 1970's did the village of today take shape with the renovation of old properties and the creation of a country park with Wycoller at its centre. An eerie timeless atmosphere still pervades the centre of this pretty little village.The ancient **bridges** of Wycoller Dean are an attraction in themselves. Near the hall ruins are an old packhorse bridge and Clapper Bridge (possibly named after the sound of Weavers' clogs crossing the bridge). Further up the dean Clam bridge is a huge slab of gritstone that appears precariously balanced on either bank and is one of the oldest bridges in the British Isles (more than a thousand years old).

Boulsworth Hill is the main geographical landmark on the route; its long linear ridge parallels your journey away from Wycoller Dean.

LEGAL NOTE: Some work may have been performed on the section running alongside Boulsworth Hill by the time you cycle it.This is because a recent public enquiry upgraded parts of the section and it will now form part of the Pennine Bridleway, which has a final completion date of 2000. Therefore there may inevitably be some changes to the surface and signposting along this section but the line of the track should remain the same.

6. BLEARA MOOR

START *Foulridge Canal Wharf*   **Grid ref.** *888425*

DISTANCE *17km / 10.6 miles*   **TIME ALLOWED** *3 hours*

GRADIENT DIFFICULTY *2. The ascent to Bleara moor is 3 if tackled in the wet and 2/3 in the dry. It's best avoided anyway after rain to stop damage to the track surface which will only exacerbate the problem.*

TRACK SURFACE *On-road = 9km / 5.6 miles Off- road = 8km / 5 miles. A great variety of surfaces from excellently made canal tow path to unmarked bridleway across fields of sheep ! The only section that may prove muddy after rain is the upper reaches of Stanridge Clough Lane by Bleara Moor.*

ORDNANCE SURVEY MAPS
1;50,000 *Landranger 103 Blackburn and Burnley*
1;25,000 *Outdoor Leisure 21 South Pennines (New edition)*

ACCESS *The village of Foulridge lies grouped around the A56 less than 2km north of Colne, the latter also providing **train** access. The canal wharf is well signed off the main road and has ample parking as well as a superb cafe with home baked dishes and their own bread! Thoroughly recommended for 'refuelling' after the day's ride.*

SUMMARY *Variety is the spice of life; an adage proven by this route. A quiet canal side ride with pretty painted boats belies the drama of the climb to Bleara moor which requires some stamina; don't worry though, this is the only major effort on a route otherwise within the grasp of riders 10 years old and up. Pleasant village lanes in Earby and Kelbrook complete the picture. Foulridge Tea Rooms and Restaurant at the canal wharf is highly recommended. Home cooked food at reasonable prices ! (Summer- every day from 10 a.m. Winter - Wednesday to Sunday from 10.30 a.m.)*

Pick up the canal tow path past the tea rooms on your right in Foulridge wharf. Carry on, keeping the canal on your left, under several bridges with pretty white painted arches. On meeting the first road bridge by the Anchor Inn bear **R.** Come straight into Salterforth to meet the B6383 and straight across it. Immediately the road bears right past Salterforth post office on Earby Road. The road leads through North Holme to a T-junction with the main road in Earby (A56). **L** takes you to a **R** ¶ picnic site and youth hostel (**not** the most immediate 90 degree right of New Road which you meet at the same junction). Carry on past shops bending right past the small bus station on the left to a T-junction and **R** here again ¶ youth hostel. Shortly take a **L** down Water St. (¶ Youth Hostel) to run alongside a beck and pretty houses. Pass the Red Lion Pub and Youth Hostel to exit the village to a split in the road.

At the split go **R** to follow the footpath sign (the left leading downhill goes to a Caravan Club site). Shortly a blue arrow confirms your course on this rising track and the footpath peels away from our route to the right. Your way is obvious, passing Stanridge Clough Farm on this lane of the same name. The only possible confusion lies just ahead where a track into a field on the left should be ignored in favour of a green 'ditch' of a track, waymarked on a wall, and hemmed in by stone walls on either side.

Climbing on this difficult section pass through a bridleway gate into an open field and follow the wall on your right with the heather of Bleara Moor just the other side. It's worth taking these tricky upper parts slowly, in any case, to appreciate the fine views behind and to your left, over the start of the Pennines. Aim for the ruined building ahead and pick up the obvious wide green lane, bounded by walls, behind the building. Follow it to a T-junction with a minor tarmac road where a mast is seen in front of you.

R onto this road to another 'T' and **R** again as the Pennines start to rise on your left. Starting to descend take the first **R** just past Broom House Farm and continue past 'Out Laithe' to take the next ¶ **0** on the **L** just before Cocket House. The track leads downhill to the front of Harden Old House. Go round the left side of the house and cut across the field behind the house and through the only gate. Bend 90 degrees **R** and follow the edge

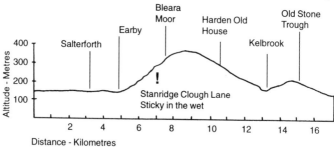

34

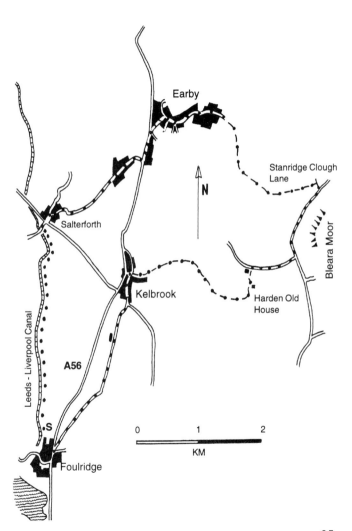

Earby

Stanridge Clough
Lane

N

Salterforth

Bleara Moor

Leeds - Liverpool Canal

Kelbrook

Harden Old
House

A56

0   1   2

S

KM

Foulridge

of the field and a small brook on the right to pass through the gate in the corner of this field. Do the same in the next field, passing Harden New Hall, visible a few hundred metres away on the other side of the valley. Here cross over the brook which has turned sharply left to join Harden Beck in the valley bottom. Straight on into the next field where Pendle Way markers (a witch) and a **0** waymarker (in the opposite direction) confirm your course over this field to a gate next to a large stile. Continuing over the next field Copy House looks down from the valley side, up to your right. Finally end the field section by crossing over the next field, under telegraph wires, to a covered water tank, and straight onto the excellent track leading you into the back of Kelbrook in about 1km.

The track crosses a small bridge over Harden Beck in Kelbrook to meet a minor road. Go **R** to meet Main Street and **L** onto it to head away from the church. Shortly, by the post office, take a **L** up Waterloo Road. Climbing, stay on this road past Yellow Hall and into the hamlet of Old Stone Trough. Follow this dipping minor road for another couple of kilometres, into the back of Foulridge, and take the first minor **R** down the steep Stony Court and cross the main road down Chapel Steps. Past the Hole in the Wall pub the Wharf is signposted.

ALONG THE WAY

Foulridge Wharf *is an interesting starting point. Look out for the Lime Kiln here, where lime was quarried for lock construction in the 1790's. At the very start of the towpath look back to see the end of the Foulridge Tunnel coming to the end of its 1640 yd length. In 1912 a cow fell into the canal at the other end and decided to swim through the tunnel. The incident is recorded in the Hole in the Wall pub (see directions). Although inaccessible by bike there are organised trips through the tunnel on the boat 'The Marton Emperor.'*

As well as housing the usual collection of pubs and cafes the village of Earby also boasts the **Museum of Yorkshire Dales Lead Mining.** *Although not particularly relevant to the area covered on this route it provides a good excuse to visit the Old Grammar School, a fascinating building in its own right, where the collection is stored.*

Ascending Bleara Moor *yields superb views. Contrast the gentle slopes of White Moor behind you to the increasingly dramatic vistas of the start of the Pennines towards Skipton on your left.*

7. PENDLE HILL

START *Downham village*　　　　　**Grid ref.** *785443*

DISTANCE *31km / 19.3 miles*　　　**TIME ALLOWED** *5 hours*
Note there are a number of shorter and
easier options as detailed below.

GRADIENT DIFFICULTY *3 if the whole 31km is tackled, but a moderate 2 if all the easier options are taken.*

TRACK SURFACE *On-road = 19km / 11.8miles Off-road = 12km / 7.5 miles. The surfaced roads are generally small and quiet, the only real exception being the road from Pendleton Hall up to the Nick of Pendle. The quality of bridleway varies from extremely technical to easy flat green track. Consult the alternative route descriptions and try to judge if you can handle the conditions described.*

ORDNANCE SURVEY MAPS
1;50,000 *Landranger 103 Blackburn and Burnley*
1;25,000 *Pathfinders 669,670,680,681*

ACCESS *From the Burnley, Nelson, Colne conurbation there are a number of minor roads over Pendle Hill to Downham to the north. From Skipton Downham is on the A59 before Clitheroe.* **Car** *There is a car park in the south west of Downham near a visitor centre and toilets. Clitheroe* **train station** *is about 9km away and Nelson some 13km.*

SUMMARY *Pendle Hill is the heart of Lancashire Hill Country and its most famous landmark. Although this route doesn't visit the famous Beacon summit or 'Big End,' at 557m (1827ft), it circumnavigates Pendle Hill and offers splendid views of the hill itself and its surroundings. It also gives you the chance to make up your own route round the hill, as alternative loops are detailed. The full 31km is quite a tough proposition in terms of distance, gradient and the terrain covered. Avoiding the longer loop options will cut the distance down to around 20km ahd avoid the most difficult terrain.*

Leaving Downham centre in a south easterly direction (away from the hill of the main street) take the **R** hand road just over the small bridge. This quiet minor road runs parallel to the north west face of Pendle Hill and passes the steep-sided Worsaw Hill on the right. Ignore several minor turns on the left until reaching one ¶ as a dead end and for Little Mearley Hall and take this **L**. The well tarmaced road ends as it bends left towards the first buildings on the track (Little Mearley Hall) and nice wide green lane takes over. Pass over a small tumbledown bridge as to the right factory chimneys at Clitheroe disturb a tranquil view, with the distinctive 'lozenge' of Longridge Fell sloping away further to the west.

Past Lane End farm on the right the green lane becomes tarmac and leads to the group of buildings at Mearley Hall. Stay on the main track bending through the buildings and through gates. The road degrades somewhat before finally leading to Pendleton Hall at a T-junction with the road. **L** here to a very steep climb to the Nick of Pendle, past the Wellsprings Inn and a ski slope.

ALTERNATIVE LOOP 1.
This loop avoids the steep climb to the Nick of Pendle, which is only for the fit. It can only be used instead of, not as well as alternative loop 2, as it uses the same section of bridleway. The bridleway itself can become very boggy indeed in places and is therefore better avoided after wet weather.

Emerging at the road by Pendleton Hall go straight across the road and follow the tarmac road into Pendleton. In Pendleton take a minor **L** to Wiswell and through this second village to the A671 and **L.** Past woods on the left take the next **L** up a minor road ¶ Sabden and bear next **L.** Follow the road as it turns to **0** past farm buildings. Follow up a long slight gradient to emerge on a road just down from the Nick of Pendle and go **R** to resume your original route.

ALTERNATIVE LOOP 2.
Coming over the Nick of Pendle after the first short steep drop look for a track on the **R, ¶ 0,** and with countryside advice on a Forest of Bowland sign. This bridleway track is the same track that brings you the end of loop 1, above. Follow it onto tarmac surface and to the T-junction at the end and **L.** Stay on the main road ignoring the right to Read. Follow this road for about 5km to the junction with the main road in Sabden. The original route enters by this main road.

Pick up the turning signed for the parish church of St. Nicholas (straight across from loop 2 or left if coming straight over the Nick). Facing the church drive, at the end of the road, head **L** down a small lane ¶ Badgers

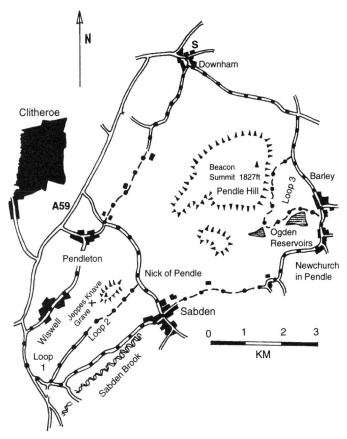

Clitheroe

A59

S

Downham

Beacon
Summit 1827ft
Pendle Hill

Loop 3

Barley

Ogden
Reservoirs

Pendleton

Nick of Pendle

Newchurch
in Pendle

Jeppes Knave
Grave ×

Sabden

Wiswell

Loop 2

Loop 1

Sabden Brook

0   1   2   3

KM

Wells Cottages. Bearing right round a corner ignore the first ¶ **0** to the right and at the next T-junction, in front of a farm house, go **R** on the tarmac ¶ **0.** The road climbs to Ratten Clough farm and through it changes to a track and starts to descend. The slopes of Spence Moor rise close by to the left. The track descends to the next building (under renovation at the time of writing) where it twists downhill and passes over a brook surrounded by trees and a farm building to climb once again. The track straightens and levels out to join the tarmac road again at a T-junction. **L** here to go through Sabden Fold farm to the next cluster of buildings at Sabden Hall. The road now climbs steeply over the lower slopes of Spence Moor to arrive at the T-junction in Newchurch in Pendle (¶ reveals you've arrived on Wellhead Road). **L** onto the main road through this tiny, pretty village to climb steeply, staying on the main road to arrive at a fine view on the crest of the hill just out of the village.

The steep descent yields superb views of the eastern flank and Beacon Summit of Pendle Hill, Barley beneath you and the hill of Aitken Wood down to the right.

ALTERNATIVE LOOP 3.

This is the most difficult loop of all. It doesn't add a great deal of distance but contains bridleway which is essentially a steep field push followed by a single track, rocky and very technical descent. Some proficiency is required to avoid falling so beware and watch your speed ! The route does offer great vistas to the east over Ogden reservoirs and brings you close to the impressively steep hill beneath Beacon End.

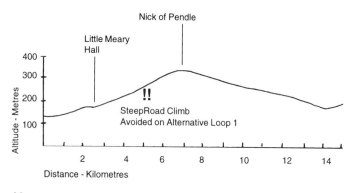

Entering Barley at the end of the steep descent take the first **L** over the bridge, ¶ to Ogden Clough and Barley Green. Follow through gateposts marked no unauthorised vehicles and past the fine Nelson Waterworks (1912) on the right. Follow the deteriorating track alongside the first larger reservoir and past a small plantation on your right. Ignore the track to the right, for Higher Buttock farm (no joke), and follow to the end of the track by 2 large metal gates. Go through the wooden **0** gate on the **R** and follow the barely discernible path by the wall on the right to the corner of the field (an extremely hard push !).

In the corner go through the gate in front of you. Ignore the next gate and stile in front of you and bear **R** through gateposts. Dropping down, negotiate the mini-ravine and pick up the bare narrow path to pass above Buttock and after a small descent above buildings at Upper Pendle. This narrow undulating path starts to run parallel to a wall on the right and maintains this course into a field behind farmhouses at the base of Beacon Summit. All the while are superb views of the undulating country to the right and Pendle Hill to the left. In this ultimate field ignore the 'yellow witch' signs leading you away and to the summit. Proceed straight across the grass to the right hand corner of the field and through the gate and **L** onto the road. This road joins the original route at the main road.

To avoid this very hairy route simply follow the main road through Barley, with fine but admittedly less spectacular views than the loop. About 3km out of Barley take a **L** at a minor crossroads. Simply follow this fine road section for 4km to return to Downham, with the Ribble valley landscape to your right and the 'narrow end' of Pendle Hill to the left confirming your final steps 'home.'

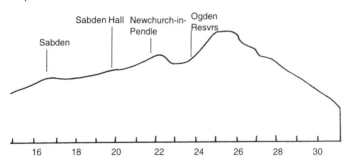

ALONG THE WAY

Downham *is a pretty, quiet village, thankfully not submerged by the effects of tourism. There are a wealth of residences from Tudor, Jacobean and Georgian times and the local nobles, the Asshetons, have left their mark in both the village church in the form of relics and as a coat of arms on the pub. The village has convenient facilities including a cafe, car park, information centre and toilets. See Whalley Abbey details in 'The Nab' route for more details about the Asshetons.*

Pendle Hill *is of course inseparable from the area's links with the Pendle Witches. The famous Beacon summit derives its name from fires lit on this point, which have acted as signals throughout the ages. From medieval military rallying calls or warnings of Scottish raids to modern day celebrations of the jubilees of Victoria and Elizabeth II, the Beacon Summit has seen it all. The witches themselves were seventeenth century residents of local villages. Their trial centred on the mutual hostility of two local families headed by the 'witches' Demdike and Chattox. They were executed after a brief trial in August 1612. Although this is an undoubtedly true story there is little evidence of these happenings left today; just the tourist legacy of Pendle Witch pubs and local tourist paraphernalia. Every Halloween a crowd gathers on Pendle Hill in celebration of these dark events.*

Newchurch in Pendle *is home to a church with a couple of quirky features; the 'eye of god' carved on the tower mystically gazes over the town's inhabitants whilst the grave marked 'Nutter' is marked with skull and crossbones; nobody appears to know exactly why! Tearooms and toilets in the village may provide a welcome break. Also look out for the 'Witches Galore' shop.*

Stonyhurst College (Route 16)

8. BRADFORD FELL

START *Waddington*   **Grid ref.** *729439*

DISTANCE *18.5 km / 11.5 miles*   **TIME ALLOWED** *3.5 hours*
Shorter loop option = 15.5 km / 9.6 miles

GRADIENT *A hard 2 if Rodhill Lane is included but an easy 2 if you take
the shorter option.*

TRACK SURFACE *On-road = 10.5 km / 6.5miles Off-road = 8 km / 5
miles. The long uphill section to Bradford Fell may be a 'ride some push
some' section, depending on the time of year and your ability. Parts of the
fell traverse may be 'sticky' out of summer but after this the track is excellent.
The Green Lane down to Rodhill Lane track can be very wet at the start but
soon passes over well-drained field sections (see legal note on possible
change).*

ORDNANCE SURVEY MAPS
1;50,000 *Landranger 103 Blackburn and Burnley*
1;25,000 *Pathfinder 669 Clitheroe and Chipping*

ACCESS Cars *may park in the village of Waddington 2 minutes north of
Clitheroe on the B6478. There is also a **train** station in Clitheroe.*

SUMMARY *You will feel the long ascent to Bradford Fell well worth the
effort as you gaze over the Ribble Valley to the distinctive outline of Beacon
End. Also look out for fine views of Pennine limestone country to the north
on the road section over Beacon Hill. Such scenery together with the pretty
village of Waddington mean you can easily turn this into a leisurely, interest
-filled day, perhaps stopping in Sawley for refreshment or sight -seeing.*

Heading north through Waddington turn off **R** for West Bradford, just after
the Methodist Church. The eyesore of the quarry workings of Clitheroe
blemish the impressive outline of Pendle Hill to the right as you ride out of
Waddington passing the old hospital on the left as you leave. Coming into
West Bradford take the first **L** ¶ Eaves Hall and as a dead end, and pass a
very elegant country club. The well made track continues to the ¶ for
Seedalls. Here the good road bears left but you carry straight on through a
gate to green track in a field, ¶ **0**. Follow the line of the green lane through

gates. The gradient flattens out to cross the moorland of West Bradford Fell. Shortly after a right- left bend in the track bear 90 degrees right to traverse the moor, the track edge initially being marked by wooden boards (don't be tempted to go straight on through two old stone gateposts). Follow this track, more or less on the level, to a T-junction at the end by a plantation (possibly felled by the time you ride this section!). Go **R** downhill to shortly emerge through a gate and bear **R** onto the stone track. This undulating track- cum -road passes the odd shaped Shimpsey Hill to the right with good views before emerging at a road T-junction.

(SHORT OPTION AVOIDING THE FIELD SECTIONS OF RODHILL LANE:
At this T - junction go **R** and descend for about 1km. Immediately as you begin to enter the village of Grindleton take the first unsigned **R.** Descend and pass over Grindleton Brook in the bottom of a small valley then climb steeply. Ignore the first **0** on the right and passing farm buildings follow onto the well-made track, a continuation of the tarmac road. The track becomes green lane as it bends left to follow the woods of West Clough Brook to the right. Descend to pass the impressive residence of Green Banks on the right, rejoining the tarmac at this point. Rejoining the main road at a T-junction at the bottom of the descent turn **R** to and stay on this road through West Bradford and back to Waddington).

IF TAKING THE LONGER OPTION:
L onto the road and climb to further Ribblesdale views on the right. Shortly after passing Scriddles Farm on the left the road begins to level out then descend. Take the easy to miss ¶ **0** on the **R,** situated on a left-hand bend, as the Pennine limestone country opens out in the distance. Follow the **0** between walls and downhill. Although partly overgrown and badly drained, you ignore the first pedestrian gate into a small field and soon head off **R,** through the first vehicle gate and into a large field. Follow the left hand side of this field which has the remains of some type of edifice on the mound in the middle of the field. Going through the gate at the end of this field the eyesore of the quarry at Clitheroe comes into view down to the right. Follow the faint track of a green lane, more or less straight on, through the middle of the next field. On meeting the brow of the hill magnificent views over the Ribble and its Pendle Hill backdrop come into view; you can spend quite a while identifying many features on the valley floor and the hills to the north-east on your left. The green lane becomes better defined to descend quite steeply to the end of the field and apparently ends at the fence.

Turn 90 degrees to the **R** here and coming into the next field look for the

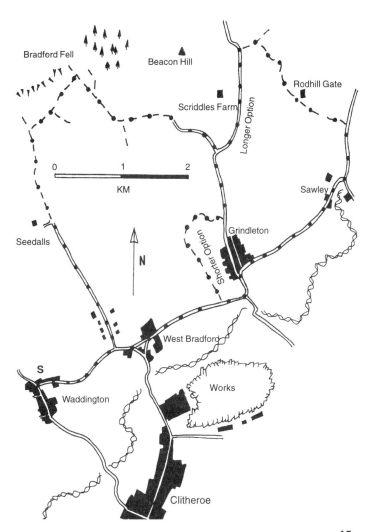

Bradford Fell

Beacon Hill

Rodhill Gate

Scriddles Farm

Longer Option

0   1   2

KM

Sawley

N

Grindleton

Shorter Option

Seedalls

West Bradford

Works

S

Waddington

Clitheroe

45

start of a steep -sided green lane, its entrance guarded by small twisted oak trees (stile and footpath waymarkers show a footpath crosses the top of our intended route). However the green lane itself is illegally blocked a little way down. **Legal note; As our legal route is barred we are quite entitled to pick our own line as close as we can to the original.** Simply follow through the fields on the right of the green lane which resembles a tree-filled ditch down to your left. Eventually the fields and green lane terminate at a farm track. As your way is blocked here lift over the fence and bear **L** onto the track, shortly passing Rodhill Gate on the left. Descend the track to meet the road at the bottom and **R**. (Note renovation work to open up the closed section of bridleway is planned sometime in the future).

At the next T-junction just before Sawley Bridge take the **R** turn ¶ Waddington, Grindleton and West Bradford. It's then simply a matter of following this road for a further 6km back to your starting point in Waddington, ignoring any turnings on the way.

ALONG THE WAY

Waddington not surprisingly often features in the stakes for the county's best kept village, but even without beautification and the superb Coronation Gardens contains much of interest. The church of St. Helen's is complemented further up the main street by the compact Methodist church and its unusual tower. The Old Hall boasts an historical connection for it is

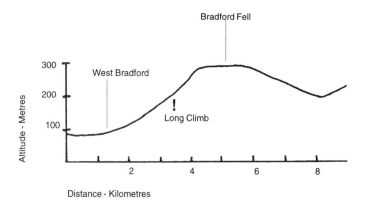

here that the periodically insane Lancastrian king, Henry VI, spent a night in 1464 after his defeat at the battle of Hexham during the Wars of the Roses. The ambiance is completed by two pubs and a tearoom, giving you ample excuse to stay and contemplate the charms of this small gem of a village. There are further opportunities for pub stops in West Bradford and most notably in Grindleton at the 300 year-old plus **Buck Inn.**

The village of **Sawley** is easily visited, lying right next to the route after your descent down the track of Rodhill Lane to the Ribble Valley. Its historical 'showpiece' is the ancient ruins of Sawley Abbey. Now in the possession of English Heritage they are open to the public. The history of these crumbling stones mirrors closely the story of their grander neighbour at Whalley (see route 18, 'The Nab'). Similarly founded by Cistercian monks the abbey suffered the same fate during the dissolution and the abbot of Sawley Abbey was likewise hanged for support of the 'Pilgrimage of Grace' rebels, protesters against the effects of Henry VIII's radical religious policies. Refreshment conveniently awaits you in the village pub.

View-wise perhaps the view over the Ribble from the brow above **Rodhill Lane** is the finest prospect, affording views not only over the immediate valley but of the South and West Pennines to your left. Earlier as you begin to ascend this bridleway section **Ingleborough and Pen-y-ghent** stand proud in the northern distance.

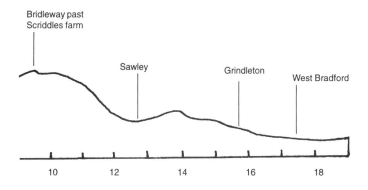

9. SALTERS WAY

START *Slaidburn village*   **Grid ref.** *712523*

DISTANCE *24km / 15 miles*   **TIME ALLOWED** *3.5 hours*

GRADIENT DIFFICULTY *2. There are several short but steep grade 3 climbs on the ascent. However it's worth pushing up these if you don't have the extreme fitness to pedal them, as they give access to miles of gently undulating track on Salter Fell and above the River Roeburn.*

TRACK SURFACE *On-road = 10km / 6.3 miles Off-road = 14km / 8.7 miles. Most of the off-road surface is good quality green lane or well drained rocky, wide track, making for easy off-road riding. However a relatively small section in the middle may become very muddy in the winter months.*

ORDNANCE SURVEY MAPS
1;50,000 *Landranger 103 Blackburn and Burnley*
          Landranger 97 Kendal to Morecambe

ACCESS *The village of Slaidburn is approached from Clitheroe on a beautiful road, through the villages of Waddington and Newton or is a short hop from Long Preston on the A65. The small village centre has a car park near the Youth Hostel. **Train** Clitheroe station is about 13km from Slaidburn and Wennington about half this distance from the finishing point of Hornby.*

SUMMARY *Although linear this route has been included as it has been described as one of the finest moorland crossings in England. The views both ascending and descending are superb and contrast strongly with each other. It is however relatively long and needs suitable clothing as, even on a fine day, you may find cold winds increasing the chill factor at altitudes*

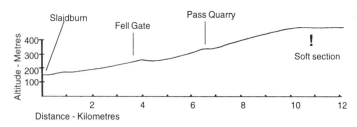

around 400m (1300ft). You could split the route into two day rides if returning to a car is vital, riding to a suitable vantage point then retracing your steps, though this won't enable you to sample the glorious change of scenery from south to north, achieved in completing the full distance. A fine day is vital to make the most of the superb views.

Entering Slaidburn passing the church proceed up the road and **L** in front of the Hark to Bounty inn. Just before exiting the village up a small steep climb there is a pretty weir a short walk away from the road on the right. Continue out of the village on this undulating minor road to pass Ellerbeck Hall on the left with the steep side of Burn Fell ahead of you. Take the first **R** up Woodhouse Lane (¶ dead end for motor vehicles). The road passes through several farm settlements and rises to meet the fell gate.

Through the gate the road has a concrete surface. Bending left round the edge of Low Fell the beautiful valley housing Croasdale Brook opens up before you. Follow the obvious course of the road as you see it dip (over a bridge) and rise to a quarry on the left. Steeply climbing past the quarry the track then levels out for some distance before a gate heralds a muddy section suffering from deep troughs formed by vehicles. On the section prior to the gate look out for a shooting box on the left and Great Bull Stones at the far side of Croasdale Brook, on the right.

You find yourself on a bleak plateau, effectively a pass between the higher fell areas either side, as the steep sided valley housing the Whitendale River runs away to the south on your left. Passing very close to the valley head, the level landscape then meets a gate to rejoin well surfaced track and the increasingly steep drop to Mallowdale on the left amidst a boulder strewn landscape. After a brief glimpse along a length of the river Roeburn the track heads away from the dale edge to round a smaller valley that joins Mallowdale. The farmhouse at High Salter comes into view on this section and it is here you rejoin a minor road.

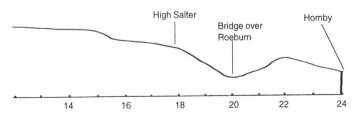

From the farmhouse it's simply a matter of following this road for several kilometres into Hornby. It dips and climbs steeply to cross the River Roeburn and pass over the slopes below Whit Moor. It's then an effort-free downhill run to your finishing point in the Lune Valley, crossing straight over the B6480, to meet the main road through the village. If aiming for Wennington railway station take the only right turn off the descending road, ¶ Wray, picking up the B6480 in this village, leading you to the station.

ALONG THE WAY

Slaidburn *is a compact village ideal for exploring the much under-rated Forest of Bowland. It is centred around a Youth Hostel and the Hark to Bounty pub. The latter was originally the home of the forest courts and the panelled court room is preserved upstairs. Further attractions include St. Andrew's church, with its origins in the 15th century and a village green, post office and cafe.* **Wray,** *near the end of the route boasts cobbled streets and Tudor and Jacobean architecture. Its unfortunate position on the confluence of the Roeburn and Hindburn left it exposed to floods in 1967 that ripped away many of its bridges, walls and cottages. The focal points of the other possible finish point,* **Hornby,** *are the river Wenning winding its course through the centre and the castle, mainly of 19th century construction. Though the latter is now a private residence it can be viewed from the bridge.*

The Cross of Brown is the base of an ancient cross, one of a number lining an ancient monastic route. Look for it at the start of the drive to Mytton Farm Crafts, just after turning down Woodhouse Lane on the first part of the route.

Three Peaks Country, along with **Morecambe Bay,** *can be seen on the latter stages crossing Salters Fell; over the flat area of Godber Common to your right you will be able to identify the outlines of the Three Peaks of Whernside, Ingleborough and Pen-y-ghent.*

Grouse are reared and shot over much of the area; note the turf emplacements for shooters ascending the side of Croasdale Brook. The distinctive Black Grouse with its red eyebrows is a common sight.

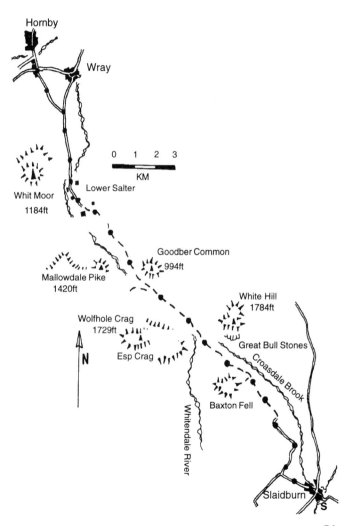

Hornby

Wray

0 1 2 3
KM

Whit Moor
1184ft

Lower Salter

Goodber Common
994ft

Mallowdale Pike
1420ft

White Hill
1784ft

Wolfhole Crag
1729ft

Great Bull Stones

Esp Crag

Croasdale Brook

N

Baxton Fell

Whitendale River

Slaidburn
S

51

10. THE RIVER RIBBLE

START *Bolton-by-Bowland village*   ***Grid ref.*** *786495*

DISTANCE *32km / 19.9 miles*   ***TIME ALLOWED*** *4-5 hours*

GRADIENT DIFFICULTY *A relatively easy overall 2. The route aims to follow the Ribble as closely as possible, so no prolonged gradients are encountered.*

TRACK SURFACE *On-road = 20km / 12.4 miles Off-road = 12 km / 7.5 miles. A real mix of all types of off-road track; wide, well-made farm tracks, green lanes and field sections give the aspiring mountain biker a good opportunity to experience just about everything. The bottom part of the track down to Forest Becks should be avoided after wet weather as it easily becomes a natural channel for water. Instead of turning onto it at Monubent Head you can carry straight back into Bolton-by-Bowland on the road.*

ORDNANCE SURVEY MAPS
1;50,000 *Landranger 103 Blackburn and Burnley*
1;25,000 *Pathfinders 660,661 with small sections on 669 and 670.*

ACCESS *Close to the A59, Bolton-by-Bowland has its own car park.* **Train** *Clitheroe station is about 10km away.*

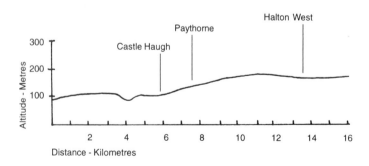

SUMMARY *The Ribble gently snakes its way south of Bolton-by-Bowland and this ride gives you the chance to encounter it, in its many forms. It is quite enchanting, from the more dramatic views from the old castle mound at Castle Haugh to the wide green plain near Cow Bridge and its impressive Pennine backdrop. Wildlife abounds; I've spotted curlews, deer and hare all on this route.*

From the car park in Bolton-by-Bowland head through and out of the village, passing the church on the left. Follow this road for 4km until dropping down to a bridge over the Ribble, ignoring minor left turns on the way. Bear **L** here, uphill on a track, ¶ **0** and 'Private, No Access to Hospital', by the BASC buildings. Ignore the left leading to the back of the hospital buildings and proceed over the cattle grid to carry straight on, ignoring the right turn just past the gate. Shortly pass through a bridleway gate and take the middle option of the three choices in front of you, to cross over the tarmac road and descend to cross over the bridge of Stock Beck. Follow the track as it bends left away from the house and climbs to go through stone gateposts. The track improves in quality and shortly meets the A682 main road.

At the first main right hand bend after turning **L** onto the main road look for a ¶ **0** on the **L**. Head diagonally over the field aiming at the tree covered mound on the far side, following further signs for the Ribble Way. There are fine views from the castle mound. Go through two bridleway gates at the mound to follow the field downhill to a wood entrance, keeping by the fence on the right hand side. Enter the wood through the bridleway gate and follow the good dirt track to emerge at a road bridge over the Ribble.

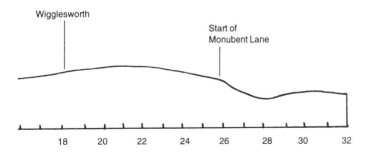

Turn **L** over the bridge and stay on the road through Paythorne. At the end of the long straight leading out of the village a ¶ **0** carries on the straight line of the road, so turn **L** onto here. After a short track section it becomes a green lane overgrown with trees. Soon the limestone country of the Pennines comes into view to the right. An alternative way can be followed in the fields to the right, as, in any case, the lane is sealed off part way down. However, further up bridleway gates, of recent construction at the time of writing, lead you in a straight line through fields to emerge on a road.

R here to shortly cross the first set of crossroads and keep on this road to approach Halton West. Just as you enter the village go **L** at the first group of farm buildings, **0** ¶ Deep Dale, up a good farm track. Pass a left turning, following straight on ¶ Ribble Way. Approach Low Scale farm and follow over the stile to the left of the farmhouse and into the field. Follow the edge of the field by the farm buildings and a barn further on, to another stile. Don't go over the stile but turn **L** to follow the fence on your right. A stone wall appears ahead of you; cross the end of the field to go through a gate opposite and meet the end of a farm track. Heading **R** on the track will lead you through the middle of High Scale Farm, picking up the hard surfaced road past the farmhouse on the right. Follow to the B6478 road.

Bear **L**, away from Cow Bridge which crosses the Ribble, as Ingleborough rises proudly in the distance. Entering the tiny village of Wigglesworth ignore the minor road joining from the right. If you look back on the road section before Wigglesworth you'll also be able to see steep sided Pen-y-ghent. Shortly after a minor right take the next split **L**, ¶ Bolton-by-Bowland and Sawley. Shortly turn **L** ¶ Paythorne. Pendle Hill comes into view on this section, along with Pen-y-ghent and Ingleborough, enabling a rare view of all three at the same time. Pass a radio mast and left turn for Hellifield to come to a crossroads.

R here ¶ Bolton-by-Bowland and shortly after a left turn for Gisburn and opposite the next set of farm buildings, take a **0** ¶ Forest Becks on the **R**. A good track leads past a house to **0** gate on the right. Follow through this to go down a wide green lane which leads to another **0** gate. Through here the track narrows and decades of neglect have produced quite a magical tree- filled gully where pushing may well be required. Meet a track at the bottom and bear **R** and immediately bend left over two bridges in succession to emerge at the road in Forest Becks hamlet. **L** here leads you down the

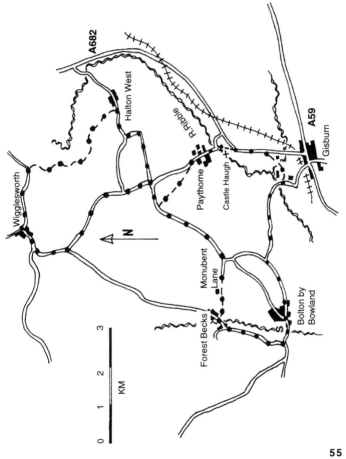

western side of Bond Beck and the next **L** at the T-junction brings you back into Bolton-by-Bowland.

ALONG THE WAY

Bolton-by-Bowland *is an idyllic spot, boasting two village greens, a post office and a fine church. The latter has a splendid 15th century tower and inside you can find a 1460's carved stone memorial to a local nobleman, his 3 wives and 25 children ! Also look out for the decorated font.*

This route offers tantalising glimpses of **Pennine limestone country,** *whilst never actually crossing over to the river's eastern side to travel into its midst. Each exceeding 2000ft, the summits of Ingleborough and Pen-y-ghent flank the southerly course of the Ribble down the eponymous dale. The rich strong greens of the grass that flourish on limestone stand out on a bright summer's day, whilst the surreal limestone features of pavements and scars combine with the verdant pasture to give this* **Three Peaks Country** *its unique character.*

The Crook O' Lune (Route 11)

11. LANCASTER-GLASSON

START *Lancaster, New Quay Lane.*   **Grid ref.** *470623*

DISTANCE *25km/ 15.5 miles*   **TIME ALLOWED** *2.5-3 hours*

GRADIENT DIFFICULTY *A very flat 1.*

TRACK SURFACE *On-road = 5km / 3.1 miles   Off-road = 20km / 12.4 miles. The Lancaster-Glasson cycleway is purpose made and generally good quality. The bridleway sections are also generally easy with the slight exception that the ultimate 'green lane' section before rejoining the cycleway is rather bumpy. All minor roads are quiet outside of bank holidays.*

ORDNANCE SURVEY MAPS
1;50,000 *Landranger 97 Kendal and Morecambe and 102 Preston and Blackpool*
1;25,000 *Pathfinder   648   Lancaster and Morecambe and 659   Galgate and Dolphinholme*

ACCESS *For access onto New Quay Road in Lancaster by car or from the city centre **train station** see Lancaster town centre map.*

SUMMARY *On this route the River Lune contrasts completely to the up-river sections featured in the Caton Moor route; here it retains the feel of a sea estuary, broad and wide with plenty of wildlife. A medium length run ideal for a relaxing family outing.*

Follow New Quay Lane to its end, passing alongside the Lune on the right. At the road terminus a cycleway continues on in the same direction (also ¶ as **0**). Continue on the main cycle track until meeting a tarmac road on your left leading to Aldcliffe. Don't follow this road but bear **R**, as you face down the road, taking you through a **0** gate and following signs for the Lancashire Coastal Way. After following the Lune estuary closely on the right and open pasture on the left, you pass the beautiful Meldham Wood on the left, masking Ashton Hall.

Shortly after this pass through Conder Green picnic area (a small concrete road section with toilets) before rejoining the cycle track. Don't make the mistake of following the road from the picnic site into Conder Green. Cross over the River Conder bridge and shortly the track terminates with a broad green stretch of grass on entering Glasson, opposite Glasson Marina.

At the Victoria Inn swing **L,** over the end of the B5290 to cross a small bridge over the water link between the marina and dock, with accompanying traffic lights and lock gates. Climb out of Glasson to Tithe Barn Hill and stay on the main road. Drop downhill to a sharp left hand bend. Ignore the dead end straight ahead at the bend (actually to Old Glasson) and turn **R ¶** Lancashire Coastal Way. At the end of a track go through a **0** gate to follow the distinct line of a green track over fields, which ultimately ends at the farm buildings ahead of you. In front of these buildings pick up the hard surfaced track to the left and follow it along the seafront, as the Lune estuary opens out to join Cockerham Sands in front of you.

On meeting the tall metal tower by the cottage turn **L** back onto surfaced road and to the T-junction at its end. You may wish to detour right here to visit Cockersand Abbey (for details see below). This unusual edifice is found down the first farm track on the right, but note this track is a footpath only. The abbey is clearly visible behind Cockersand Abbey Farm. Otherwise go **L** at this T-junction and continue on past the first left turn for Glasson. The hills of the Forest of Bowland rise ahead of you in the distance.

Shortly watch out for a rough track on the **L, ¶ 0.** Follow the track through a gate and proceed through a couple of fields, in a straight line, passing one good farm track on the right. Coming to what is effectively a T-junction with a green lane between fields go **L** onto it. Follow this bumpy track to its end at the minor road and go **R.** Take another **R** at the next T-junction taking you over the canal and to the B5290 in Glasson. The cycleway you followed on your outward leg is on the other side of this road. Use it to retrace your steps to your starting point.

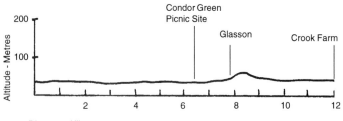

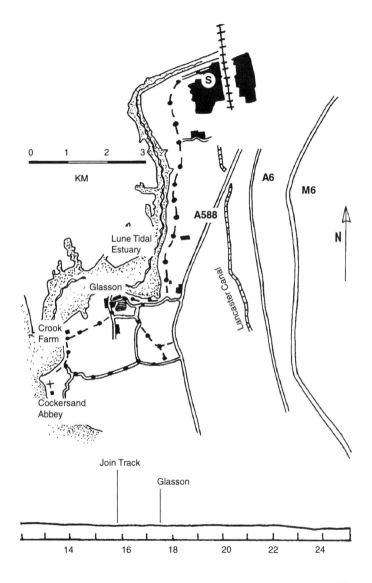

0   1   2   3
KM

S

A6

M6

A588

N

Lune Tidal
Estuary

Lancaster Canal

Glasson

Crook
Farm

Cockersand
Abbey

Join Track

Glasson

14   16   18   20   22   24

ALONG THE WAY

Commencing the route look out for the **Maritime Museum,** facing the Lune on your left. The 1764 Custom House has been restored to provide a wealth of displays on topics as diverse as the city's trade with the West Indies and North America and the fishing industry of Morecambe Bay.

The Lune Estuary hereabouts is protected as a Site of Special Scientific Interest. The marshes support a huge population of worms and invertebrates which are a tasty food source for the thousands of birds that flock here.

The Cycleway follows the line of the former Lancaster-Glasson railway. There was once a station at Conder Green and the line itself linked up to the main Preston to Carlisle line. The Station Master's house in Glasson and the Crossing Keeper's cottage at Conder Green still remain. Passenger and goods services were eventually halted in the 1930's and 1940's respectively.

Glasson Dock was built as an 'overspill' from the port of Lancaster whose Lune estuary could no longer handle the increasing size of ships, due to silting up. It was funded by Lancaster merchants in the 18th century and the Lancaster Canal was extended here in 1826. This meant ships in port could load directly onto canal barges. The dock is still commercially operated but nowadays the majority of craft here are leisure cruisers, moored in the Marina.

Cockersand Abbey is an easy, minor detour from the main route. Originally a monastic cell, cut off from the outside world by marshland later drained, it was subsequently enlarged to become St. Mary's of the Marsh and one of the richest religious establishments in Lancashire. In the 12th century a hospital for the sick and leprous was founded and by the fifteenth century the abbey had its own quay for those arriving by sea. The only part to survive Henry VIII's dissolution of the monasteries was the still remaining Chapter House, preserved as it was used as a burial place. It is thought the monks at this abbey built the first lighthouse on the coast here.

12. CATON MOOR

START *Lancaster Castle*   **Grid ref.** *473619*

DISTANCE *28km / 17.4 miles*   **TIME ALLOWED** *3.5-4 hours*

GRADIENT DIFFICULTY *Generally a level 1/2 but with a 2/3 climb to Caton Moor requiring basic fitness.*

TRACK SURFACE *On-road = 12km / 7.5 miles Off-road = 16km / 9.9 miles. The Lancaster-Caton cycleway is, for the most part, well surfaced and very flat. The only real climb comes on the minor road ascent to Caton Moor, preceding a steep off-road descent suitable for riders with at least some experience of such conditions. There's also a small amount of urban and 'A' road cycling.*

ORDNANCE SURVEY MAPS
1;50,000 Landranger 97 Kendal to Morecambe
1;25,000 Pathfinder 648 Lancaster and Morecambe 637 Burton-in-Kendal and Caton

ACCESS *Park in Lancaster town centre for access to the Castle (see town centre map on pg.65). The **train** station in Lancaster is a couple of minutes from the castle.*

SUMMARY *Largely flat and suitable for semi-beginners this route does feature one tough climb and a descent where good brake technique is required. Combined with the length this means some basic cycling experience is advisable.*

From the SW corner of the Castle descend steeply down Long Marsh Lane. Just before the railway bridge over the road turn **R** down an unmarked track, in fact the Lancaster-Caton cycleway. Immediately pass Vicarage Field on the right with Priory Church sitting above it. Follow through Lancaster, passing behind Sainsburys and going under a subway under Greyhound Bridge Rd. and into Green Ayre Park (see town centre map, pg.65). In this small green area head under Skerton Bridge, keeping the Lune on the left. You are soon on the cycleway proper and leaving the city behind.

Look out for a large impressive weir on the left then the army training base on the opposite bank shortly before passing under the large concrete M6 motorway bridge. There are then superb views of Halton church and surrounding desirable residences, just across the Lune. Cross a minor road and through a car park area to eventually cross the old railway bridge over the broad, forested banks of the Lune. Then immediately passing under a road bridge you are confronted with a number of splits; take the left-hand most option into a car park with toilets. (It's worth carrying on at this junction to the next railway bridge to take in the superb view down the Lune before heading back to actually take the correct turning). Head to the road and **L** to cross back over the road bridge above the cycleway, then over a longer bridge over the Lune itself. Hit the main A683 road and go **L** into Caton. At the first roundabout in Caton go **R** ¶ Brookhouse and Littledale.

Stay on this road through Caton and over the bridge into Brookhouse. Just before the Black Bull Inn in Brookhouse turn **R**, ¶ Moorside and Littledale. Very shortly take a minor **L** over a small bridge down Moorside Rd. Climb on this road to the first small settlement and take the first unsignposted **L** on a right hand bend. This climb becomes increasingly hard but with increasingly fine views over the Lune valley to the left. Follow the road to its end by a windfarm and the remains of an old quarry.

Through the gate simply follow the rough track, passing the ruined building on the right, and dropping to pass under aerial ropeways that carry containers to and from the clay works on the right (they connect the clay workings with the brick factory in Claughton).There are magnificent views as described below from Caton Moor above the clay works. After rounding the source of a stream you find yourself set for the descent to Claughton on a grass track and entering a field by a plantation. Keep the plantation on your immediate left to descend another field in similar fashion to find a rough track beyond the left hand of two gates. Watch your control on this track.

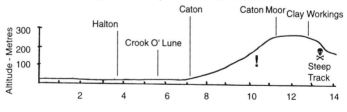

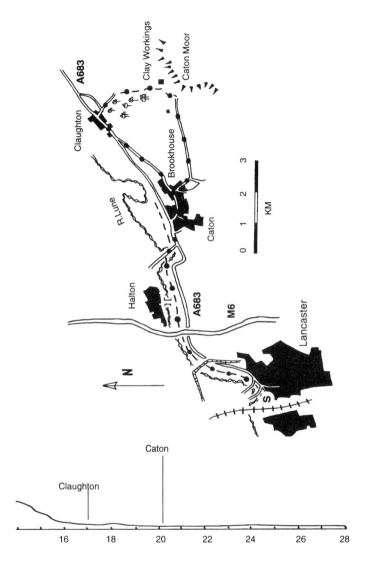

Finish descending the track to bend right through a gate as the track levels out. Keeping on the obvious track join a tarmac road, ignoring a left here for Claughton Hall, the splendid residence up to your left. Descend the road and through a bridleway gate to finally leave the woods behind. Coming to the A683 in Claughton go **L** by the Fenwick Arms. Take the next **L** off the main road ¶ Brookhouse and Littledale. Pass through the former settlement and Caton to the roundabout, again going **L** to join the A683. Shortly on the **R** the next turning takes you over the Lune to the familiar car park from where you rejoin the cycleway back to Lancaster.

ALONG THE WAY

The cycleway to Crook O' Lune *follows the trackbed of the former Lancaster-Wennington railway. In its heyday it linked Lancaster with the main line station of Skipton and was extended to the small coastal village of Poulton. This latter settlement soon became a fashionable newly- named bathing resort, Morecambe, taken from the ancient name of the sands. In the 1960's the line was closed to passengers and visitors from Leeds heading for Morecambe now had to go via Carnforth. The 1970's saw the total closure of the line with the axing of the freight service.*

*On the cycle track coming out of Lancaster you'll also pass under the impressive **Lune Aqueduct**. 600ft long and 60ft high it's the product of the 18th century engineering genius of John Rennie. It's incredible to think that the man who was also a moving force in the construction of London, Waterloo and Southwark bridges, London and East India docks and Bell Rock Lighthouse began work as a millwright and had no formal training as an engineer !*

*The **Crook O' Lune** is the long 180 degree bend where your journey on the cycleway ends. It's beauty was remarked upon as early as the mid-eighteenth century by Romantic poet, Thomas Gray, in his guide to the Lakes. Before arriving here on the canal path observe **Halton churchyard** on the opposite bank of the river, housing a Norse preaching cross which served as a place for worship before the church. .*

*The views from **Caton Moor** are ravishing. Pennine peaks to your right compete for your attention with a beautiful prospect over the Lune, whilst to your left Morecambe bay shimmers and Lakeland Peaks rise up behind.*

LANCASTER CITY CENTRE
For route location when starting routes 11 and 12

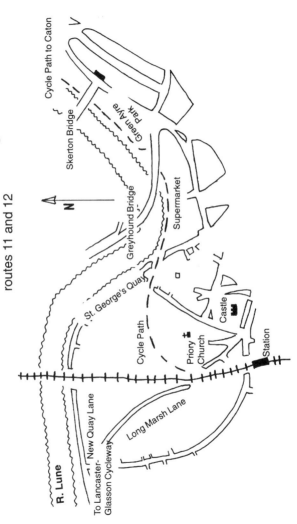

Cycle Path to Caton

Skerton Bridge

Green Ayre Park

N

Greyhound Bridge

Supermarket

St. George's Quay

Castle

Cycle Path

Priory Church

Station

R. Lune

New Quay Lane

To Lancaster-Glasson Cycleway

Long Marsh Lane

13. SILVERDALE

START *Warton village*   **Grid ref.** *498723*

DISTANCE *26km / 16.2 miles*   **TIME ALLOWED** *3-3.5 hours*

GRADIENT DIFFICULTY *2. Occasional steepish climbs are never too long and are broken up by flatter sections, reflecting the fact that this area is a blend of coastal topography and moderate forested hills.*

TRACK SURFACE *On-road = 14.5 km / 9 miles   Off-road = 11.5 km / 7.2 miles. Quiet minor roads are complemented by bridleway tracks of generally excellent quality over wooded limestone hills, typical of this small corner of Lancashire. The bridleway along the coast at Silverdale runs over tidal flats so to avoid a potentially muddy track high tide is best avoided. However at other times it's perfectly fine.*

ORDNANCE SURVEY MAPS
1;50,000 *Landranger 97 Kendal to Morecambe*
1;25,000 *Pathfinder 636 Grange-Over-Sands*

ACCESS *Warton is located just west of the A6 and M6 (off Junction 35), about 15km north of Lancaster. Carnforth* **train** *station is a few minutes ride from Warton, and a branch line goes up through Silverdale and Arnside.*

SUMMARY *For connoisseurs of unique landscapes this route of medium difficulty and length is perfect. Extensive salt marshes border a number of craggy limestone knolls which provide a good introduction to off -road climbing.*

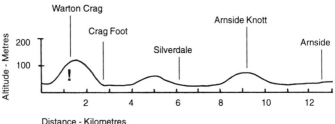

Starting from the Church Hall and the Parish Church of St. Oswalds in Warton head towards the centre of Warton up the main road. Take the first minor **L** past the post office, ¶ Coach Road and to Leighton. Climbing out of Warton the hills beyond the M6 appear to your right. Just by Potts Cottage take a ¶ **0** for Crag road on the **L**. The hardest climb on the route takes you through deciduous woodland but soon levels out to pastureland broken by limestone outcrops.The track then drops through further woodland to emerge at a road. There are excellent views over Siverdale's coastline.

R onto this road and keep descending into the hamlet of Crag Foot, to meet the main road at a T-junction. Go **R**, ¶ Silverdale and Arnside, and follow the road over a level crossing to another T-junction. **L** here, ¶ Silverdale, and climb through woods. Take the next turning **L**, ¶ Wolf House Gallery and Jenny Brown's Point, onto Hollins Lane. Ignore the next minor left, for Jenny Brown's Point (dead end), as you enter Silverdale. At the village T-junction go **L**, ¶ the shore (the village centre including shops, post office and tourist information can be found to the right at this junction). The road ends at the foreshore. Continue onto the foreshore and pick up the trail as indicated by the signpost in front of you, ¶ 'The Cove' and the Lancashire Coastal Way. A faint but obvious track sticks close to the cliffs of the National Trust property of The Lotts on the right. The track finishes at the cove by a cave in the cliffs, just beneath a castellated wall. Join the tarmac road to your **R** through a **0** gate and climb to a T-junction.

L, ¶ Arnside, heralds a beautiful coastal ride with views over the Kent Channel, before the road turns inland to approach the distinctive wooded outline of Arnside Knott. The ruins of Arnside tower come into view to the right of the road. Opposite the farm track that descends to the farm in front of the tower take the **0** on the **L**, ¶ Arnside Knott, with further signs showing

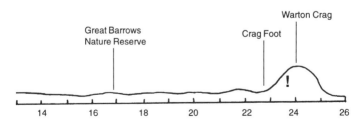

you it's a National Trust property. Follow the main track through the woods, ignoring any minor turnings and following any signs for Arnside. Emerge into the car park and join the road at the end of the track leading out of the car park. Pick out the Kent Viaduct ahead as you descend on the road to a T-junction and **R**.

Now in Arnside village pass the Youth Hostel on the left to meet the T-junction with Silverdale Road and **R**. Pass a bakery and several small shops and take the next main **L**, just past the Church of Our Lady of Lourdes. Drop steeply down to a T-junction and **R**, ¶ Silverdale and Carnforth, to cross a level crossing. Take the second **L** up Storth Road. Just as you enter Hazelslack go **R** down a broad track, ¶ footpath to Leighton Beck, although it's actually a byway. This excellent track passes through yet more woods to a T-junction with a road.

R onto the road to a further T-junction, just over Leighton Beck. Go **R** here and ignore the next right for Arnside and Milnthorpe. After passing through the woods of Gait Barrows Nature Reserve emerge to and cross over yet another level crossing. Stay on the main road to pass Silverdale station, but note shortly after this there is a left ¶ Leighton Moss and Yealand you should take if you wish to visit the nature reserve (see 'Along the Way'). Take the next **L** ¶ Warton and shortly after crossing over the level crossing take a familiar **L** up Crag Road, ¶ Warton. A toughish climb takes you back to the **0** on the **L**, Crag Road, which you can use to follow your outward steps back to Warton.

ALONG THE WAY

Warton Crag and Arnside Knott are typical of the small limestone hills in this area. It's incredible to think the limestone of these small hills was being formed 300 million years ago when the area was a warm sea, teeming with the skeletons of corals and sea lilies that deposited themselves to become this soft, porous, white rock. One geological theory is that, during the last ice age, these hills were small islands in a vast lake that occupied the site of Morecambe Bay. Warton Crag was used by Celts for the construction of a strategic fort and later it became a warning beacon, for example to warn of the invading Armada. **Warton Village** itself counts the Washington family, whence came the first president of the U.S., amongst its more notable progeny.

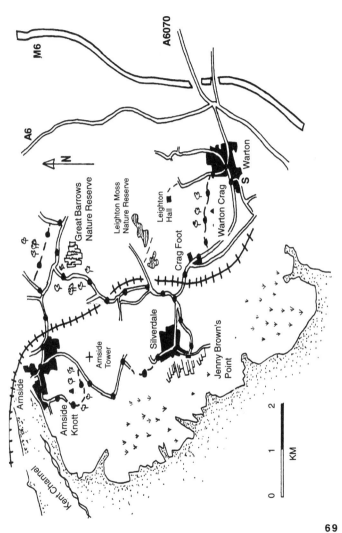

Silverdale is a pretty, compact village, not overly affected by the moderate number tourists who visit. It's famous in the literary world as the Victorian novelist Mrs. Gaskill spent time at Lindeth Tower (see map for location). The nearby Wolf House is said to be where the last wolf in England was killed, during the reign of Edward I. The town's main industry was previously cockling and shrimping.

Just off the route, but definitely worth a visit, are **Leighton Moss RSPB Nature Reserve** and the nearby **Leighton Hall**. The former houses many rare bird species and otters can also be spotted in the lakes there. The latter, a beautiful limestone hall, is set in its own grounds, being the home of the Gillow furniture- making family whose furniture is on display within. It also includes gardens with a maze and a birds of prey display. Open May-July inclusive and September, 2.00 - 5.00 pm. August only 11.30 am - 5.00 pm. Admission charge made. For location of both attractions see the route map.

Unusual coastal scenery at Silverdale (Route 13)

14. TROUGH OF BOWLAND

START *Chipping village*   **Grid ref.** *413434*

DISTANCE *28km / 17.4 miles*   **TIME ALLOWED** *4.5-5 hours*
            (Shorter loop - 20km/ 12.4km)

GRADIENT DIFFICULTY *The climb over Whins Brow makes this a very serious grade 3. I wouldn't advise anyone of whatever ability to try the descent after Whins Brow whilst mounted ! The smaller loop is a difficult 2.*

TRACK SURFACE *On-road 12km / 7.5 miles Off-road 16km / 9.9 miles. This run varies from the very easy 'road' by the River Dunsop (technically off-road as it's not open to traffic) and the incredibly hard push over Whins Brow and the following hairy descent. The push over Whin's Brow is certainly not recommended in the wet or in bad weather conditions. Occasional field sections increase the stamina required.*

ORDNANCE SURVEY MAPS
1;50,000 *Landranger 103 Blackburn and Burnley*
1;25,000 *Pathfinder 669 Clitheroe and Chipping 660 Slaidburn and Forest of Bowland*

ACCESS *There is a car park in Chipping, to the west of the centre, past the church on the right. Clitheroe **train** station is some 13km away.*

SUMMARY *Easily one of the most spectacular routes in the book, and the full route is certainly the hardest, Whin Fell being for serious mountain bikers only. For me the two outstanding views are over the Hodder valley, emerging from the plantation whilst passing under Totridge and the incredible view over the Brennand valley coming down Whin Fell. Even if you opt for the easier route there is consistently fine Bowland scenery.*

From the car park head back through the village, past the church on the left and between the Talbot Inn and the Tillotsons Arms. Take the first **L** by the war memorial onto this quiet country lane and pass the first ¶ **0** on the left at Leagram Hall Farm. Fine views of Longridge Fell on the right accompany you here. Look out for the next ¶ **0** on the **L** just as you exit the farming hamlet of Leagram Mill. Follow this good track past the distinctive rocky outcrop of Knot Hill on the left to pass through Lower Greystoneley farm and immediately descend into woods as the track becomes rockier. Passing over a beautiful ford climb out of the woods and follow the obvious track through Higher Greystoneley Farm and to a T-junction with the road.

After a **L** here you'll pass a dead end with a telephone box on the left, bending right on the road to climb past the rocky ridge of Long Knots. Shortly after you have climbed and you begin to drop take the next **L**, ¶ as no access for motor vehicles and as a **0**. This excellent quality farm track soon leads you past Tungstall Ing and to a split. Head **R,** away from Higher Fence Wood farm a short distance away on the left. Shortly a **0** is ¶ with a waymarker and hand-written sign to lead you off the good track and up a green track to the **R** (by a cluster of chicken sheds). Shortly reach a gate at the edge of a plantation and follow the only path through it to emerge at the other side by a beautiful drop down a green lane, and superb views over the Hodder valley on the right. Descend on the green lane to a wood and follow waymarkers through the trees to ascend to a **0** gate into a field. Head down across the field and through the gate by the stile at the other side, into an even bigger field, with the hump of Mellor Knoll in the field to the right. Follow the wooden waymarker posts across the middle of the field, towards the left hand side of Mellor Knoll.

Soon a bridlegate and stile come into view in the corner of the field. On reaching these head downhill through the **0** gate and follow the good track. In the next field the good track is lost but continuing down over this and the next field simply follow a line down to bridlegates which become apparent part way down each of the fields, to emerge on a track by a white cottage in the valley bottom. Head **R** here to cross over a small bridge and bear **L** over a larger bridge to rejoin the road at a T-junction.

(**SHORTER LOOP ALTERNATIVE.** You are now at the start of the famed Trough of Bowland which extends up the valley to your left. If you don't want to face the mighty challenge of Whin Fell ahead of you go **R** here and follow the road down valley and bear **R** at the next junction, just on the edge of Dunsop Bridge. Pick up the directions at the point marked * below).

Going **L** here, for the harder Whin Fell option, continue up the valley through the hamlet of Sykes to a small sign 'Tarnbrook', by a barn, indicating mountain rescue equipment is no longer to be found in the barn. Going **R** follow the rocky track above a wooded bank and round a plantation to eventually pass through the middle of crumbling buildings. Continue on the track towards the middle of the horseshoe shaped ridge ahead. The surface

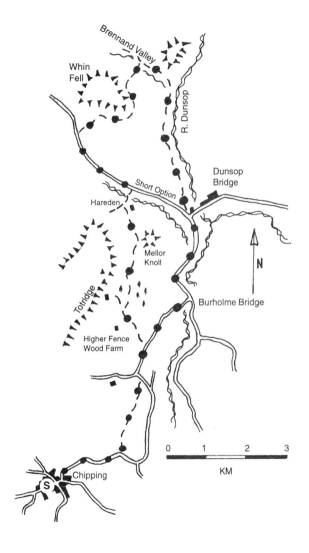

Brennand Valley

Whin Fell

R. Dunsop

Dunsop Bridge

Short Option

Hareden

Mellor Knoll

N

Totridge

Burholme Bridge

Higher Fence Wood Farm

0   1   2   3

KM

S

Chipping

becomes green track which you follow by a wall on the right which soon bends away to the right. Carry straight on, on the faint narrow path, a challenging push over a huge field to the stile and gate at the other side. There are impressive views of the rolling fells on the other side of the Trough, behind you.

Through the gate follow the left side of a shaly ravine ahead and to the left. After a very hard gradient levels out a marker post leads you to a thin path to follow a fence on your right and to a gate and stile. All across the tops layers of moorland extend to the distance and Fountains Fell is now prominent ahead. Follow the narrow peaty track ahead and suddenly a superb view of the Brennand Valley opens out beneath you. The track narrows further as it swings left to a steep descent, eventually to a **0** gate, after a hair-raising descent. **Do not attempt to ride this- push carefully !** Head across large and small fields in succession. Although the line of the **0** is indistinct here head for the back of Brennand Farm. Head **R** once in the farm buildings to pick up the road that follows the Brennand river. Follow the road as it swings right, heading south, to follow the River Dunsop on your left.

Meeting the next T-junction the heart of Dunsop Bridge village is down to your left. Turn **R** away from the village and keep on the main road, avoiding the next right, ¶ Lancaster. * 2.5 km on, after following the course of the Hodder, turn **R** before Burholme Bridge onto a minor road ¶ Chipping. A climb and a drop past Long Knots brings you to the recognizable dead end and phone box on the right. Shortly after this the farm track leads to Higher Greystonely. **R** down here gives you another chance to sample this glorious section of **0** and to retrace your outward steps back to Chipping.

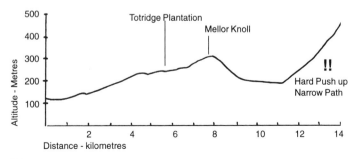

ALONG THE WAY

Chipping once had as many as five mills all driven by the nearby brook. Nowadays the most visible is the cornmill converted to a restaurant on the main street. It also has a good collection of pubs and a church, restored in Victorian times. The 17th century school and almshouses are amongst the most interesting buildings. For refreshment try the Cobbled Corner Cafe, a veritable haven for cyclists at weekends ! All this is set amidst a small and idyllic stone-built village.

Dunsop Bridge is a very short detour off the actual route (see map). Although it can become excessively crowded during summer weekends and other 'peak times' it remains a quiet attractive, tiny village at other times. Its quirkiest feature is its telephone box; have a look for yourself and find out why ! Its pretty green lies alongside a river and on its western edge it boasts St. Hughbert's church, the latter being the patron saint of hunters and protector against mad dogs!

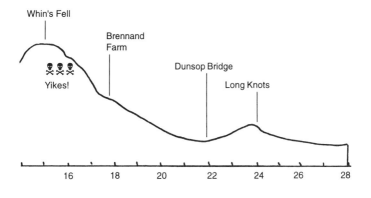

15. GRIZE DALE

START *Beacon Fell Country Park*   ***Grid ref.***   *573427*

DISTANCE *33km / 20.5 miles*   ***TIME ALLOWED*** *4 hours*

GRADIENT DIFFICULTY *This is a hard 2, not because gradients are excessively steep but there are quite a number of moderately testing gradients on this long route.*

TRACK SURFACE *On-road = 27km / 16.8 miles Off-road = 6km / 3.7 miles Although the vast majority of this route is on quiet minor roads the off-road sections at Beacon Fell Country Park and at Grize Dale are well surfaced and drained and should be easily negotiable by riders of all abilities.*

ORDNANCE SURVEY MAPS
1;50,000 Landranger 102 Preston and Blackpool
1;25,000 Pathfinder 668 Garstang

ACCESS *The start point of Beacon Fell Country Park is easily reached by car from the main north-south road arteries of the M6 and A6, to the west, and is less than 20km from Preston town centre. Unfortunately, although the **train** line goes north from a major station at Preston, passing quite close by Beacon Fell, there is no station between Preston and Lancaster.*

SUMMARY *The considerable length of this mainly minor road route is more than compensated for by the superb contrasts you encounter. Views over the Bowland Fells from Beacon Fell Country Park and over the Plain of Lancashire from beneath Grize Dale Fell are the perfect complement to the wooded and watery tranquillity of Grize Dale itself.*

Park in the eastern-most car park of Beacon Fell Country Park, amongst trees, just off the 'ring road' that encircles the park and just north of a tarn. The country park is a maze of tracks and roads. The park authorities are quite happy for bikers to use any of the well surfaced vehicle width tracks that run through the forest. I have suggested a way westward through the park using the map of the fell, sampling the view from the summit on the way, but use the map to find your own way through (directions through such a complex system of tracks would be excessively complicated).

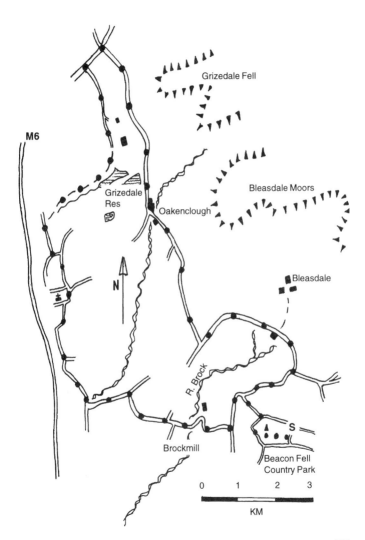

M6

Grizedale Fell

Bleasdale Moors

Grizedale
Res

Oakenclough

Bleasdale

N

R. Brock

Brockmill

Beacon Fell
Country Park

S

0   1   2   3

KM

Emerging from the forest onto the road at the western end of the park follow the clockwise direction of the 'ring road' and exit onto the first unsigned **L**. Descend the minor road to a T-junction and **R** heading for Parlick. Take the next turn **L** ¶ Bleasdale, Oakenclough and Garstang. Pass the picturesque Bleasdale post office with a cafe nearby. After subsequently crossing the Jack Anderton bridge take the next **R,** ¶ Lancaster and Oakenclough.

After crossing the foot of Bleasdale moor drop to cross over the River Calder in the tiny settlement of Oakenclough (ignoring minor left here), then climbing to magnificent views over the Lancashire Plain and Morecambe Bay to the left (look out for Blackpool Tower and the peaks of the Lake District further to the right). Finally, 5km after Oakenclough, go **L** at the crossroads. Pick up the first unmarked **L** onto a very minor road. Cross a ford and stay on this road in a straight line to reach a gate, ignoring the road as it swings left to terminate at Fell End Farm. Go through the gate (¶ 'Public Bridlepath, No Vehicular Access'). After several gates on this obvious well made track you enter beautiful woods, then come alongside the quiet depths of Grize Dale Reservoir. Continue on the track through Pedder's Wood to emerge again at the road.

Go **L** on to the road and to a T-junction. **L** here to climb by more woods on the left to another T-junction. **R** here (left is a dead end to Burns Farm). Emerge through another set of woods at a T-junction with a pretty church visible down to your right and bear **L**. Ignore left and right turns to come to a T-junction after running fairly close to the noisy M6. Head **R** then very soon take the first **L** ¶ Bleasdale and Chipping (straight on would have taken you over the M6). Take the second **L** turn, just over the bridge at Sandholme Mill, ¶ Bleasdale and Chipping again. Pick up the **R,** ¶ Preston 12. Beacon Hill and Parlick welcome you on the final leg of the journey.

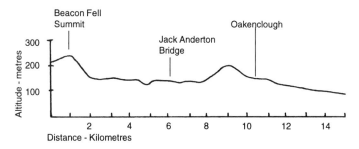

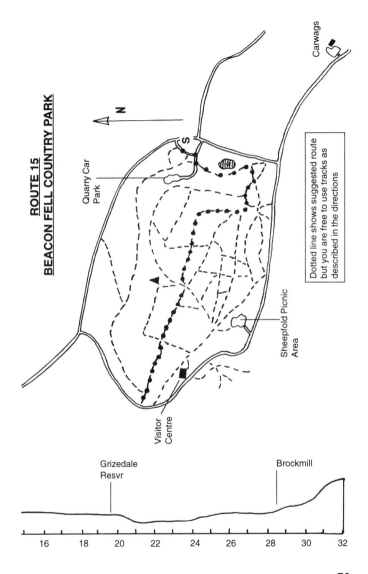

ROUTE 15
BEACON FELL COUNTRY PARK

N

Carwags

Quarry Car Park

Sheepfold Picnic Area

Visitor Centre

Dotted line shows suggested route but you are free to use tracks as described in the directions

Grizedale Resvr

Brockmill

16 18 20 22 24 26 28 30 32

Ignore left and right turns to carry on the minor road for Brockmill, ¶ as unsuitable for heavy vehicles and prohibited for buses. Passing over the delightful Brockmill Bridge you soon come to a T-junction. Go **L** and pick up the next ¶ **R** to Beacon Fell and follow the ring road at the top, back to the car park.

ALONG THE WAY

Beacon Fell Country Park *is a Countryside Commission country park and within the Forest of Bowland Area of Outstanding Natural Beauty. Its name comes from the beacon once used to communicate messages from the summit, for example the impending danger of the Spanish Armada in 1588. As mentioned, the park authorities are happy for you to bike on tracks within the park of a good surface. The Fell Side Trail (blue arrow waymarkers) was specifically set out for mountain bikers. A map of the various trails and rights of way within the park is available from the information office. One of the most pleasant refreshment stops comes shortly after your start at* *Bleasdale Post Office* *which also houses a cafe.*

The beautiful wooded *Grize Dale* *houses a reservoir for part of its length. Originally named Gris Dale, 'gris' meaning wild pigs, this beautiful secluded spot is one of the highlights of the route.* *Fair Snape Fell* *and its smaller sister* *Parlick* *really represent the south western edge of the high Bowland fells. The former, at 510m (1673 ft) is one of the few Bowland summits over 500m. The best view of both is gained from Beacon Fell summit. Views from the foot of Grize Dale Fell, after Oakenclough, can be contemplated for ages, as the flat Plain of Lancashire stretches away to* *Blackpool Tower* *and the shimmering sea. Also look out for the modern block of Heysham power station and the Lakeland fells rising in the distance.*

Lakeland peaks from above Grize Dale (Route 15)

16. RIBCHESTER

START *Ribchester*

Grid ref. *651353*

DISTANCE *25km / 15.5 miles*

TIME ALLOWED *3-4 hours*

GRADIENT DIFFICULTY *Our chosen area is delineated by the settlements of Longridge, Ribchester and Hurst Green. It's an area of undulating hills that fall away towards the River Ribble, thus providing numerous grade 2 climbs interspersed with flatter sections. Ideal for those looking for a step up from beginner level.*

TRACK SURFACE *On-road=13km / 8 miles Off-road=12km / 7.5 miles Bridleway sections are generally of good quality, some tarmac, some farm tracks, with only the occasional easily navigable field section linking farm houses.*

ORDNANCE SURVEY MAPS
1;50,000 Landranger Blackburn and Burnley
1; 25,000 Pathfinder 680 Longridge and Great Harwood

ACCESS *Ribchester village centre by the White Bull Pub.*

SUMMARY *The quaint settlement of Ribchester provides the main human interest of the route whilst the road along the base of Longridge Fell provides the widest panoramas of the landscape. Beware; a couple of 'carries' mean you should confidently be able to 'shoulder' the bike.*

Starting in front of the White Bull pub in Ribchester proceed **R** at the fork here to pass a pretty row of cottages. Carefully turn **R** onto the busy 'A' road and go over a stone bridge, looking out for the next **L** turn, ¶ Hurst Green. This quiet road soon begins to climb and in just over 2km meets the B6243 at a T-junction. Very shortly after going **R** here take another **R** down a small tarmac track (¶ **0**, but this isn't immediately obvious from the road). On meeting the first settlement of Grindlestone House follow the **L** split and descend the tarmac track. Shortly after the next buildings of 'Clough Bank' a ¶ leads us off the main track through a gate and onto a **0** on the **L,** following down the left hand side of a field to a small footbridge where a carry is necessary. Once over the bridge follow the right-hand side of the field to its end and over a stile, ¶ Ribble Way (the gate here was illegally blocked at the time of writing). Stay on the right of the next field and over a similarly marked stile to the next gate after which you pick up a rough track, noting the elegant bridge down to the right over the Ribble.

Passing through the buildings of Trough House the track becomes tarmac, climbing to eventually reach a T-junction with the road in Hurst Green. Bear **R** into the village and first **L** at the war memorial opposite the Shireburne Arms, going past the Bayley Arms Hotel and **L** down a ¶ **0** just before the entrance to Stonyhurst College (itself worth a visit, see 'Along the Way'). Once on the **0** the track splits immediately. Follow the **R** hand option to run above a glorious wooded ravine down to the left. On entering the wood a stream accompanies you on the left before you take a bridge over it then **L** at the uphill split. Follow your course out of the woods and to its end with a better constructed farm vehicle track and **R**, also a **0**, soon passing Greengore Farm (see 'Along the Way').

Passing the farm the track narrows to run alongside Deer House Wood on your right, and after its end keep on following the vague line of the track ahead to a **0** gate onto the gravel track at the other side, soon becoming a green lane leading to Crowshaw House from where a tarmac track brings you to the road. (Note the appearance of the bony spine of Pendle Hill to the right on this latter section).

L at the road junction and simply follow this road for about 5km, passing over the crossroads at the Newdrop Inn on the way, with grand views over to the left all the way. When a reservoir appears below and to the right you drop to its corner and exit the road **L** on a **0** track, ¶ Knowle Green. The initially good wide surface quickly becomes bumpy single track after a stile (gate illegally blocked at time of writing), widening again near the bottom to come to a T-junction with a tarmac track. **R** here to shortly meet another 'T' with the B6243 and **R** again. Follow this road past the south side of Spade Mill Reservoir to a T-junction at the Corporation Arms pub and **L** here.

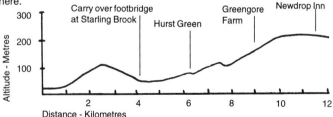

The next **R** will lead you down Hothersall Lane. Stay on this road for roughly another 4km, ignoring the only left turn on the way, to arrive at the elegant residence of Hothersall Hall. Shortly after joining the dirt track after the hall go **R** through a gate just before the track bends left, ¶ for the Ribble Way. A push uphill is required here, all the while aiming for the left hand side of the copse of trees atop the hill. Just before the trees you can follow a narrow path through their left hand edge and emerge to follow the edge of the woods downhill to a **0** gate. Now simply follow the edge of the River Ribble on your right until you join a clear track straight ahead. This takes you to a junction with a private road at the southern tip of Ribchester (the church appears over to the left at this point). Follow straight on through the farmyard to pick up the road (the Church and Roman Museum are left on joining the road and the Roman Baths straight on down a footpath by the river). The road then leads back to the White Bull.

ALONG THE WAY

St. Wilfrid's Church, Ribchester *is a beautifully proportioned church with features from numerous periods; a probable Norman door arch, a 14th century tower and eighteenth century box pews, whilst fragments of glass in the tracery window are all that remain of Puritan attacks on the church after the Civil War.*

Roman Museum. *The church and neighbouring museum actually occupy part of the site of Bremetennacum, a Roman fort established here in AD79, originally of wood and later upgraded to stone. The remainder of the site has been washed away over the course of the centuries by the river. Amongst others auxiliary troops from Asturias (in what is now northern Spain) guarded this strategic river crossing in the name of the empire. The most amazing artefact in the museum itself is a copy of a splendid helmet found by the river 200 years ago. The nearby* ***Roman Baths*** *show a more*

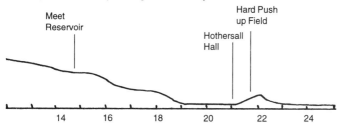

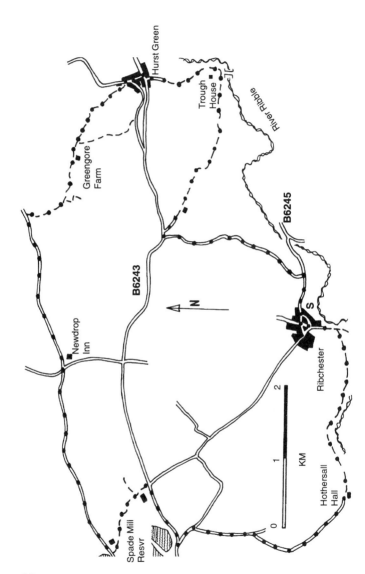

relaxed, sophisticated aspect of Roman society in Ribchester; an information board explains the complex system of underground heating and steam filled rooms of different temperatures that allowed Romans to indulge in their own concept of bathing, so different from ours.

Stonyhurst College is currently a Catholic boys' school but has a long history and the seemingly perfectly conceived approach to the facade from Hurst Green reflects different influences over many generations. The hall dates from the sixteenth century when it began life as the home of the local aristocrats, the Shireburnes. In the eighteenth century it passed to the Jesuit order as a college. These 'religious stormtroopers' of the Catholic order were expelled from a college in France and spent years here in scholastic endeavour. There are tours of the interior (Jul 22 - Aug 26) and the gardens are open to the public from July 3 to Aug 26 (both Sat-Thurs only). Enquiries 01254 826345.

Nearby **Hurst Green** is a pleasant, quiet spot luckily with a profusion of pubs. Also look out for the unusual **Alms Houses** on the right as you turn off the road before Stonyhurst College.

Greengore Farm, passed after Hurst Green, is a former royal hunting lodge where Henry VII is reputed to have stayed. It also has a camping barn, sensitively converted and offering excellent facilities and value for money. Ideally placed for exploring the mountain bike routes in the area.

Dean Farm, Sabden Valley (Route 17)

17. SABDEN VALLEY

START Whalley

Grid ref. 732362

DISTANCE 16.5 km / 10.3 miles

TIME ALLOWED 2-3 hours

GRADIENT DIFFICULTY The toughest climb on this overall grade 2 route is to the Nick of Pendle. After this there are no notably hard, extended gradients. An initial climb out of Whalley also requires a good basic level of fitness.

TRACK SURFACE On-road = 10.5 km / 6.6 miles Off-road = 6 km / 3.7 miles. Two sections of bridleway must be negotiated; the farm track to the Nick of Pendle is good quality for most of its length, however its middle section can become muddy after rainfall and in winter months generally (it also features in the Pendle Hill route). The track along the bottom of Sabden Valley is newly-laid farm track and aggregate-covered for most of its length. The climb out of the valley appears to be an ancient road, with cobbles appearing for much of the way and providing a well drained surface.

ORDNANCE SURVEY MAPS
1;50,000 Landranger 103 Blackburn and Burnley
1;25,000 Pathfinder 680 Longridge and Great Harwood

ACCESS There is car parking in the grounds of Whalley Abbey if you wish to visit this lovely tranquil site or on 'The Sands' , the street leading you to its main entrance. Whalley has its own **train station.**

SUMMARY Of relatively modest length and difficulty, this route provides a couple of testing climbs ideal for those who want to get the main pedalling effort out of the way in the first part of the route. You may want to start out of town to avoid busy traffic and make Whalley Abbey a separate visit. Also beware of the dual carriageway it's necessary to cross just outside of Whalley (A671). Otherwise you have the opportunity to enjoy superb, quiet biking in countryside at the heart of the Pendle Witches story (see 'Along the Way').

Starting outside the abbey on 'The Sands' go towards the main road, passing the parish church on the right. Go **R** at the main road to a mini-roundabout in the centre of Whalley and **L** to lead you out of Whalley, climbing up

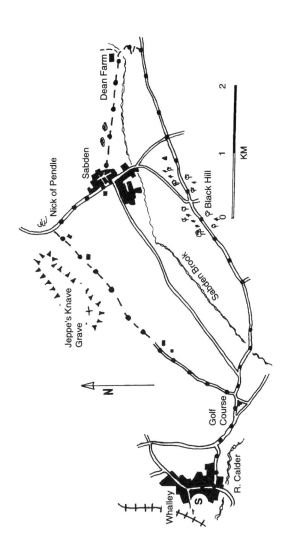

Dean Farm

Nick of Pendle

Sabden

Black Hill

Jeppe's Knave
Grave

Sabden Brook

N

Golf
Course

Whalley

R. Calder

S

KM

0   1   2

Accrington Rd. Meet the busy A671 dual carriageway and cross it, bearing **R**, then immediately take the **L** slip road ¶ Sabden. Skirting a golf club on your left enter the hamlet of Portfield and take the first **L** down a minor road, ¶ as a cul-de-sac. Passing several farm settlements the road turns to track which you follow uphill for another 2km or so to meet a public road just below the Nick of Pendle (an excellent small detour off your route as a bit of exploring on foot around the 'Nick' will yield excellent views in many directions).

Go **R** onto this road and descend steeply into Sabden village. Just past the right turn of Whalley Rd. take a **L** down St. Nicholas' Avenue. At the crossroads proceed straight over onto Littlemoor Close, the elegant church spire rising up immediately on your left. The road soon yields to a well-made vehicle track; follow its course for another 2km or so, to meet the elegant building at Dean Farm (see 'Along the Way'). Bear to the right at the farm, a bridge carrying you over Sabden Brook and onto a wide green track. This lovely track bends right then left, climbing steeply and yielding impressive views over the peaceful Sabden Valley, to meet a minor road.

Bear **R** onto this road and soon you will have equally grand views over to the left of Great Hambeldon (409m, 1342 ft) and its smaller sister Hambeldon Hill, housing a cluster of telecommunications masts. Crossing straight over the next crossroads you enter the beautiful woods that crown Black Hill (265m). Passing over another set of crossroads in the middle of the woods you will soon have the opportunity of fine views over your outward leg as you can make out the various buildings you passed on the track approaching the Nick of Pendle on the hillside over to your right.

Coming to the first T-junction after the woods take a **R** ¶ Whalley, the road dipping then climbing to take you back over Sabden Brook. **L** at the next T-junction leads you back to the A671. Bear **R** (caution - **very busy !**) and retrace your outward steps by turning **L** for Whalley off the dual carriageway.

ALONG THE WAY

Jeppe's Knave Grave, *marked on the Landranger Map as a 'non-Roman antiquity' is, according to local rumour, the grave of a notorious local criminal, Jeppe being his nickname. It is found above you and to your left as you ascend on the track to the Nick of Pendle. The name is of Saxon origin and the miscreant was supposedly beheaded during Norman times because of his repeated crimes. There is a highly plausible explanation for his unusual last resting place; unable to be buried in the consecrated ground of a church because of his offences, and neither of the local parishes wishing to have his body within their boundaries, he was buried out in this bleak spot, right on the boundary between the two.*

*This area is strongly connected with the actual events that lead to the hanging of the 'nineteen notorious witches' in 1612. It was at **Dean Farm,** passed at the end of Sabden Valley, that Hugh Moore lived. He stated on his deathbed, after a 'mysterious' illness had befallen him, that he had been bewitched by Chattox, an ancient and possibly deluded and senile woman, given to bitterly cursing the locals, who greatly feared her supposed powers.*

Whalley Abbey *is detailed in route 18, 'The Nab.'*

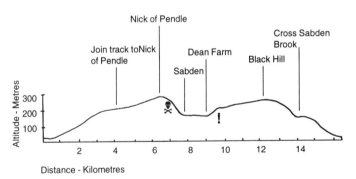

Whalley Abbey - the start of routes 17 and 18

18. THE NAB.

START *Whalley*   **Grid ref.** *732362*

DISTANCE *10.5 km / 6.5 miles*   **TIME ALLOWED** *1.5-2 hours*

GRADIENT DIFFICULTY *The initial climb up 'The Nab' merits a severe grade 3 but thereafter shorter gradients deserve no more than a moderate 2. The final descent down the bridleway overlooking Whalley needs a similarly high level of skill.*

TRACK SURFACE *On-road = 8 km / 5 miles Off-road = 2.5km / 1.5 miles. Although mainly on very quiet minor roads the bridleway sections that there are run the whole gamut of possibilities from excellent vehicle width track through rough green lane to single width, very difficult descent. Definitely for fans of variety or those wanting to experience a small taste of something new and a bit challenging.*

ORDNANCE SURVEY MAPS
1;50,000 *Landranger 103 Blackburn and Burnley*
1;25,000 *Pathfinder 680 Longridge and Great Harwood*

ACCESS *As for the Sabden Valley route (no. 17)*

SUMMARY *If this run is not sufficiently lengthy then you can simply combine it with route 17 to form a figure of eight of some 27 km or 16.8 miles. It's short, sharp and sweet, combining steep climbs and descents with stunning views over Whalley and the Calder valley. Even if you have to push your bike up the initial climb it's worth it for the bird's eye view of the viaduct over the Calder.*

As with the Sabden Valley route a good starting point is the main entrance outside Whalley Abbey. The initial directions in route 17 will direct you to the mini-roundabout in the centre of Whalley. However don't go left here as you do in the Sabden Valley route, but straight on to cross over the Calder. Just over the bridge bear **L** up Moor Lane (not the most immediate left which is a private track to 'Marjorie', a beautiful, white, riverside residence). Further up the climb look over to the right, as the Calder Valley spreads out before you spanned impressively by the brick viaduct carrying the train line north from Blackburn towards Clitheroe.

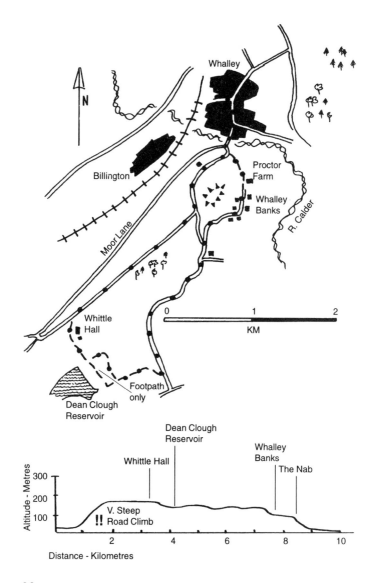

Whalley

Billington

Moor Lane

Proctor Farm

Whalley Banks

R. Calder

Whittle Hall

0   1   2

KM

Footpath only

Dean Clough Reservoir

Dean Clough Reservoir

Whittle Hall

Whalley Banks

The Nab

Altitude - Metres

300

200

100

V. Steep Road Climb

!!

Distance - Kilometres

2   4   6   8   10

As the climb begins to level out bear **R** on meeting a fork, continuing down Moor Lane. Soon you're skirting the edge of woodland; about 2km after the fork look for a track on the **L, ¶ 0,** by a stone seat. Immediately on turning don't carry straight on past the residence on the left but jink **R** up a driveway then immediate **L** to follow down the faint path down the left hand side of this field, passing trees and an outcrop of rocks to come to a gate at the end.

Through the gate descend on the green track to the corner of the reservoir ahead. Here the excellent quality track across the end of the reservoir is in fact a footpath only, so the law decrees we must take the inferior quality green lane that lies downhill, through the **0** gate just down to the **L,** at this junction of the three ways. The green track meets a small group of trees and bends off right, uphill, to meet the well-made track at a T-junction, the track having crossed the end of the reservoir above and to the right. Bear **L** here and follow to the end of the track to a T-junction with the road. Ahead are good views over the Calder Valley towards Wiswell Moor, the tail end of the long mass of land culminating in Pendle Hill at its far end.

Go **L** at this T-junction with the road. Ignore a split down Berry's Lane to the right but take the next **R ¶ '** unsuitable for heavy goods vehicles ' and a dead end. Follow the tarmac road downhill to its very end where it briefly becomes no more than single track width before passing straight through Proctor Farm. From here savour the superb views of the wooded hillside to the east of Whalley. Having picked up a well-made vehicle track just through the farm do not follow it left at the first bend but exit from it, maintaining your direction straight on down a narrow earth path, staying by the wall on the right. At the faint split the **0** goes **L** down a narrow lane defined by walls on both sides; beware of punctures here as holly leaves and brambles are numerous. This risk is reduced if you get off and push. Eventually the way becomes tarmac and shortly thereafter joins Moor Lane at a T-junction. Turn **R** here to re-cross the Calder and return to your start point.

ALONG THE WAY

Whalley Abbey *is today largely reduced to tranquil and beautiful ruins. It was originally willed by the Norman noble family the De Lacys to Cistercian monks in the thirteenth century. Its most famous resident however lived in the 16th century; the last abbot, William Paslew, was executed under orders from Henry VIII after his provision of food and shelter for participants in the 'Pilgrimage of Grace' , a popular rising in the north against the religious and* economic effects of Henry's anti-papal policies. After the dissolution the Assheton family used the abbot's house as their own residence and levelled the remainder of the abbey; rumour has it that the last act so enraged local opinion that the family were forced to move their residence to Downham because of their vandalistic approach. Modern conveniences within the grounds include parking, tea shop, gift shop and toilets.

The Parish Church of St. Mary and All Saints was founded back in the dark ages, probably by St. Paulinus around 627. There are various ancient crosses in the churchyard, including Celtic ones from the 10th century. The oldest part of the church itself is the chancel, dating from the 12th century.

The Viaduct viewed on your outward leg is locally known as the 'Whalley Arches' and is actually made up of some 50 separate arches. It's easy to appreciate what a great feat of engineering this is when viewed in its entirety from above.

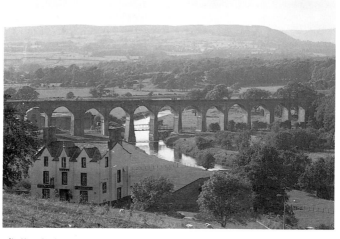

Whalley Arches (Route 18)

19. RIVINGTON PIKE

START *Lower Rivington Reservoir Car Park*   **Grid ref.** *634127*

DISTANCE *17.5km / 10.9 miles*   **TIME ALLOWED** *3 hours*

GRADIENT DIFFICULTY *There are two serious climbs to challenge you at the beginning of the route, firstly climbing out of Wilderswood and then the short but steepish ascent of Rivington Pike (although a flatter alternative is offered here). Occasional steep gradients are found on the rest of the route but nothing more challenging than an overall 2. However see summary note on varying the difficulty yourself.*

TRACK SURFACE *On-road = 5km / 3.1 miles   Off-road = 12.5 km / 7.8 miles. A veritable mountain bikers' paradise ! Good, wide hard tracks for virtually all the off-road section. Some sections may be rocky and technically very difficult, for example the descent between the Dovecote and the car park. However the majority of the tracks should be manageable by those who don't savour the 'rough stuff.'*

ORDNANCE SURVEY MAPS
1;50,000 Landranger 109 Manchester
1;25,000 Pathfinder 700 Bolton North and Horwich
Maps also available from Cycling Campaign for the North West (see introduction for details).

ACCESS *Approaching Lever Park, heading north up Lever Park Road from Horwich, park in the first car park on the left, just past the school (beware-easy to miss). Horwich itself is immediately to the north-west of Bolton. Blackrod is the nearest **train** station, about 3km from the start of the route.*

SUMMARY *Lever Park is justly popular with the locals who come here in numbers at weekends especially to enjoy the dramatic views west, as the mix of industry and rolling hills gives way to the Plain of Lancashire. It combines a surreal mix of monuments, woodland and moorland that can be explored for hours. Ideal for all, from families to experts; this route is pitched between the two but you can devise your own using a multitude of tracks.*

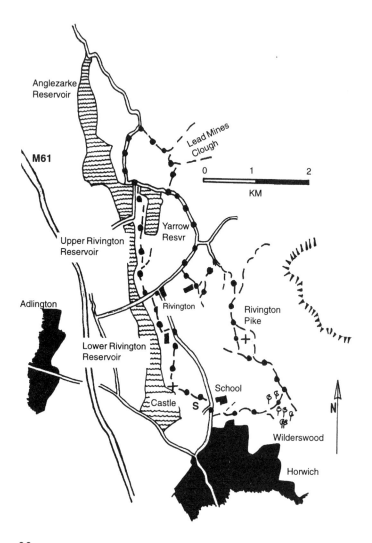

Anglezarke
Reservoir

M61

Lead Mines
Clough

0   1   2

KM

Upper Rivington
Reservoir

Yarrow
Resvr

Adlington

Rivington

Rivington
Pike

Lower Rivington
Reservoir

School

N

Castle

S

Wilderswood

Horwich

From the car park head back to the road and bear **R** onto it. Just past the school on the **L** take the ¶ **0** on the same side of the road, up the tarmac road. Shortly, just before the first bend on the tarmac road, exit down an unmarked dirt track on the **R.** Pass into a small wood and over a bridge to exit immediately and follow the track to a junction with Green Lane. **L** onto this road and climb to a ¶ concessionary **0** on the **L** and follow its initial concrete sections uphil. Impressive views open out behind you and Rivington Pike appears on the hill up to your left. Follow the track as it levels out and heads into the corner of Wilderswood ahead of you.

Here you are immediately confronted with three waymarked concessionary **0**s, taking the **L** -hand most option uphill through beautiful deciduous woods. Look out for a ¶ **0** on the **L,** appearing to join the main track obliquely from this direction. Don't be tempted to carry straight on as the track eventually narrows to extinction. Your new course winds away from the woods and after a stiff climb you reach a gate at a track T-junction. Beware as the track you join may have some slow moving traffic but this can generally be overtaken because the bumpy condition of the road limits cars' speed. There are superb views over the end of the Lower Rivington reservoir. Bear **L** on meeting this track, to head towards 'the Pike' ahead of you.

RIVINGTON PIKE OPTION; On nearing the Pike you may choose to take the **0** ¶ on the **R** which climbs towards this impressive building. This difficult cobbled track climbs behind the Pike and there is even a 'dead end' **0** split to take you to the very peak for stunning views, ¶ at the rear of the hill on which it stands. Alternatively carry straight on at the initial right turn; the track from behind the Pike joins this level track after a rocky descent. Although significantly harder the climb behind the Pike yields superb views, attaining a height of 363m above sea level.

Carrying onwards after the Pike the weird and wonderful pigeon tower is encountered. Ignore the ¶ concessionary **0** at the pigeon tower but bear leftwards down a very rocky and technical track after the Pigeon Tower. Pick up the tarmac road by the car park at the bottom of the drop and **L** 90 degrees down a ¶ **0** (ignore a **0** joining just before this, obliquely and behind you on the left). A small way down this track split **L** to pass across the head of a wooded valley, bending right to accompany the wood on the right. At the next split, just after a footpath joins from the left bear **R.** Descend to a T-junction in front of a building and bear **R.** The Rotary Club building (one of the 'barns' see below) and car park greets you just around the corner. Take the right hand most option down a green track, away from this sudden reminder of civilisation. At the end of the track meet a T-junction with a minor road.

A **R** at this junction leads to a short climb, but branch off **L** at the first junction, ¶ for Heapey and Anglezarke. A pleasant descent brings you to the bridge over the River Yarrow as it enters the eponymous reservoir. Immediately over the bridge go **R** up the ¶ public bridleway. Crossing over another bridge you soon pass the information sign detailing the history of Lead Mines Clough and the former industrial activity here - see below. After the sign bear **L** at the next split to cross another bridge and climb very steeply to leave the clough behind and pass through pastureland. A footpath and farm track join from the right as the climb levels out; bend left to stay on the main track to meet the road at a T-junction.

L here to join a long, steep descent passing a spectacular car park viewpoint on the right, looking down Anglezarke and Rivington Reservoirs. Shortly after this **_BEWARE_** of a steep drop to left-hand hairpin, potentially lethal if you aren't fully in control of your speed. After the hairpin take the first **L** up Parsons Bullough Rd, and climb to a ¶ concessionary **0** on the **R** leading in front of Yarrow Reservoir. The track joins the end of a tarmac track. Bear **R** onto the tarmac, away from the rough track leading down into woods to the left and follow to a T-junction with the public road then bear **L** away from Rivington Reservoir.

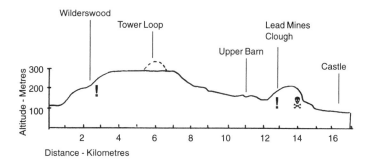

In 50m or so take the ¶ 0 to the R and head straight through the rough car parking area and pick up the ¶ for the 0, more or less dead ahead. A short section of track passes a barrier of trees in front of the reservoir down to the right, shortly to come to a children's play area on the L. Head up in this direction, passing Great House Barn Information Centre to meet the road and R onto it. Look out for the first track to the R off the road, ¶ 0 to the castle and follow the straight track to a minor crossroads, immediately to be confronted by the castle at the other side. After exploring these ruins (see 'Along the Way'), take the main track off to the L side of the edifice as you approach the castle and follow it back to the start point of the car park.

ALONG THE WAY

Lead Mines Clough is crossed shortly after your first turning off at the Yarrow reservoir. Concessionary and statutory footpaths are detailed if you wish to leave your bike and explore the higher reaches of the clough on foot. The various contraptions used to mine lead here are described. The intermittent history of mining is also detailed. A fuller information leaflet is available from the Great House Barn information centre, encountered on this route after the castle (see directions).

Lever Park is so named in honour of Lord Leverhulme, one of Bolton's most famous sons. From humble beginnings he established a business empire that was later to become Unilever, initially based on soap marketing and manufacture. This vast estate was Lord Leverhulme's private retreat but parts were also open to the public. *The Pike Tower* is a remnant of an earlier estate, built around 1773 by the then owner of the Rivington Estate and it seems it served not only to provide an even more spectacular viewing point than the summit of Rivington Pike itself, but also as a proclamation of the owner's possession of much of the surrounding land. *The Terraced Gardens* lie at the centre of the park, reflecting Lord Leverhulme's passion for landscape gardening and include such quaint features as a decorated pigeon tower and Japanese gardens amongst a host of other attractions. Unfortunately Leverhulme's residence was demolished after WWII by the new owners, Liverpool Corporation Waterworks despite local protests at this shocking example of institutional vandalism. It was a fate narrowly missed by the Pike Tower.

Perhaps Leverhulme's most innovative attempt at landscape gardening on a grand scale was the construction of an exact replica of *Liverpool Castle* as it stood, in ruined condition, just after the Civil War of the mid -

seventeenth century. Unfortunately the work was unfinished on his death. At least it has done better than the original castle which didn't survive at all ! The very first **Rivington Barns** were perhaps of Saxon origin but the two present structures date from the early 1700's. Both are visited on the route; firstly the upper barn, now housing the Rotary Club, then the lower barn, just before the castle, now Great House Barn Information Centre with an adjacent farm building being converted to a rangers' centre, craft shop and public toilets.

View over Rivington Reservoirs (Route 19)

20. RUFFORD OLD HALL

START *Rufford Village near Southport*   ***Grid ref.*** *459155*

DISTANCE *25.5km / 15.8 miles*   ***TIME ALLOWED*** *3 hours*

TRACK SURFACE *On road = 15.5 km / 9.6 miles Off-road = 10km / 6.2 miles. Easy going ! Well prepared canal tow path and road.*

GRADIENT DIFFICULTY *Canal path grade 1 but the climb away from the canal is a 2/3. You can make this an easy, almost perfectly flat, linear outing by turning back and retracing your steps at Appley Lock, covering roughly the same distance as above but without the climb (and views) of the first option.*

ORDNANCE SURVEY MAPS
1;50,000 Landranger 108 Liverpool
1;25,000 Pathfinder 699 Chorley and Burscough Bridge

ACCESS *Parking around the village centre. There is a **train** station at Rufford.*

SUMMARY *The countryside hereabouts contrasts strongly with the green, rolling pasture, typical of the Ribble further north. Large flat fields of cereals and root crops dominate the agricultural landscape. Note a permit is required for the canal section, available from British Waterways (see addresses section). The linear option is perfect for families or those wanting something undemanding in pleasant countryside. Children should not be allowed unaccompanied on the canal section as the water's edge is unguarded.*

Entering Rufford village from the north, on the A59, you may be able to park on turning **R** by the Hesketh Arms pub, ¶ Wildfowl Trust. The bike route continues down the latter turning; just past the school and the turning for the village hall on the right take the next **L** down Brick Kiln Lane, ignoring the extreme left at the same junction, named New Rd. Keep to this road, leaving Rufford behind you and coming into open countryside.

At the first fork bear **L** down Curlew Lane. Follow this narrow road to a T-junction with a larger road, bearing **L** onto Red Cat Lane here (Martin Mere wildfowl centre is 5 minutes pedalling to the right). This road leads you

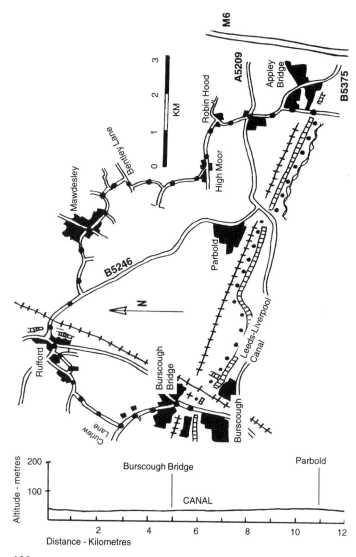

through Burscough Bridge, and 1.5 km from your turning you arrive at a T-junction with the A59. Turning **R** leads you over the railway bridge and past an attractive looking church on the left. Just before coming to the canal bridge split off **R** down Victoria St. to the canal towpath ahead. Head **L** onto the canal towpath under the bridge. There's a convenient pub by the bridge.

Once on the towpath it's simply a case of following it. It changes to the opposite side of the canal after the road bridge at Parbold (the bridge by the distinctive tower on the opposite bank; canalside tea room also here). The main highlight before this change-over is the arched bridge at the canal junction where the Rufford spur joins the canal. After Parbold it's a further 4km to Appley Lock, passing some magnificent wooded scenery on the way. **You may wish to turn back at Appley Lock and retrace your steps to Rufford,** if pursuing the easy option. If carrying on the circular route leave the canal path shortly after Appley Lock, going **L** onto the road at the bridge by the Railway pub. It's now a long, hard 2km climb to the junction with the A5209, ignoring the right turn for Shevington on the way.

Go straight over at this junction and continue into the small settlement of Robin Hood. Take the first **L** down High Moor Lane, ¶ Mawdesley and High Moor. Stay on this road through High Moor, passing a couple of pubs, and begin to descend steeply, with increasingly magnificent views over the Plain of Lancashire to the left. Look out for the next **R** down Jacksons Lane then shortly bear **L** at the next split. Coming to the T-junction with Bentley Lane go **R** and shortly take the next **L** down Moody Lane. Fork **L** to a T-junction then **L** again down Back Lane. Follow the ¶ **R** for Mawdesley village down Gorsey Lane.

Once in the quiet village of Mawdesley meet a crossroads and proceed straight over down Smithy Lane. This lane takes you to a further T-junction with the B5246 and **R** here leads you over river, level crossing and canal into Rufford, past an unusual brick church on the right. You soon meet the 'A' road you entered the village on and can easily find your way back to your start point.

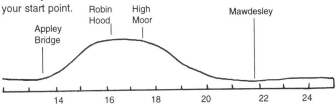

ALONG THE WAY

Rufford Old Hall is now in the hands of the National Trust. The 'Old Hall' itself is a medieval timber framed manor house with an ornate 'hammerbeam' room. It was added to between 1491 and 1523 and the east wing is a seventeenth century addition of beautiful Jacobean brickwork. A superb carved screen in gothic style, designed to cut down draughts, survives from around 1500. The residence was the home of the Hesketh family for over 700 years, many notable for their participation in military campaigns against the French and Scots. Further attractions are a folk museum showing agricultural implements and items from domestic life. The hall itself contains numerous items of furniture and artefacts ranging across the centuries. Such rich and varied attractions make it well worth a visit. Closed Thursday and Friday.

The Church of St. Mary, Rufford, is a small Victorian building in Gothic style containing many monuments to the local nobles the Hesketh family, including one from around 1458, showing 11 children.

The Leeds-Liverpool Canal passes through a great variety of scenery along its 127 mile length and hereabouts you can experience it in some of its most attractive settings, from architectural delights such as the bridge at Rufford Junction to the luscious woods approaching Appley Lock, where the flat agricultural landscape is left behind for the narrower and more natural landscape of the Douglas Valley.

Leeds-Liverpool Canal at Burscough (Route 20)